Heart-Diamond

HEART DIAMOND

For Ray and Ute and better times ahead.

Love,
Kathy

KATHY L. GREENWOOD

INTRODUCTION BY ELMER KELTON
ILLUSTRATIONS BY CHARLES SHAW

UNIVERSITY OF NORTH TEXAS PRESS

© 1990 by Kathy L. Greenwood
Manufactured in the United States of America
All rights reserved
First Edition

Book design by Kennedy Poyser
Illustrations by Charles Shaw
Cover design by Robert Opel

The paper used in this book meets the minimum requirements of the American National Standard for Permanence of Paper for Printed Library Materials, Z39.48.1984. Binding materials have been chosen for durability.

Library of Congress Cataloging-in-Publication Data
Greenwood, Kathy L., 1949–
Heart-Diamond / Kathy L. Greenwood.
p. cm.
ISBN 0-929398-08-4
1. Greenwood, Kathy L., 1949–. 2. Ranchers—New Mexico—Carlsbad Region—Biography. 3. Ranch life—New Mexico—Carlsbad Region. 4. Heart-Diamond Ranch (N.M.). 5. Carlsbad Region (N.M.)—Social life and customs. 6. Hart family. 7. Carlsbad Region (N.M.)—Biography. I. Title.
F804.C37G73 1990
978.9'42—dc20
[B]   89-21452
                                                                        CIP

The stories that follow here do not comprise the entire history of the Heart-Diamond ranch. That history is still in progress and will continue to unfold for a long time, I hope, although the small rancher, like the small farmer, is an endangered species. Rather, they are fished from the stream of my experience growing up on a working cattle ranch and offer only random samples of a way of life I believe to be unusually rewarding.

I dedicate this book to my parents, in gratitude for that experience, and to the memory of Vernon Derrick and Paul Wayne Bond.

Contents

Introduction by Elmer Kelton ix

Heart-Diamond 1

Chores 13

Cow and Bull Story 29

Roundup 41

The Voice 65

Uncle John 83

The Wild Heifer 103

Green Gate Cow 121

Going Home 149

Introduction

READING KATHY GREENWOOD'S ACCOUNT of growing up on a small ranch in southeastern New Mexico, I kept wondering where she had heard the story of my life. From her ill-starred introduction into the fine art of milking a recalcitrant Jersey cow to her uneasy homecoming from graduate school, she kept reflecting incidents out of my own West Texas experience. In many ways, she reflects the life of almost everyone—man or woman—who has grown up on a ranch.

It is a lifestyle that unfortunately is becoming increasingly rare if not actually endangered by the harsh economic facts of life. It is good that Kathy Greenwood has captured some of it for us to keep, to savor whenever we feel the need to renew acquaintance with our roots. She writes with a sparkle and a keen wit of events and situations that in most cases were not funny at the time but became funny in retrospect, after it was determined that nobody had been seriously hurt or even killed. Cowboy humor has always skirted along a fine line between the hilarious and the tragic. The nearer a situation can approach tragedy without quite crossing over, the funnier it becomes in the retelling.

She knows not only the sunny side of ranch life but the dark side as well. The most poignant chapter tells about her sister, who wanted to become a veterinarian but became a ranch wife instead, blessed with a knack for healing. She used that knack to good effect in treating a horse that had cut himself so badly the regular vet despaired of any salvation, and again in single-handedly assisting a wild but painfully pregnant young heifer with a most difficult delivery. The bittersweet outcome of these efforts pointedly illustrates the wide difference in viewpoints between her father, Hart Greenwood, born into ranching as a way of life, and a city-raised operator to whom livestock and land are nothing more nor less than an investment.

Throughout the book, the reader senses the deep attachment the rancher feels toward his land and the animals that share it with him—an attachment that sometimes clashes with the cold and practical reality of trying to make a living from them. There is, for example, the story of the Green Gate Cow, a wild Brahman that Hart Greenwood bought in the Roswell Auction and that became the terror of the Heart-Diamond Ranch. Practicality would have dictated that she be captured and resold or, if that proved impossible, shot for being a fence-busting renegade and a danger to man, woman, and horse. But practicality took a back seat to admiration for a fiery and independent spirit, and the cow was granted a lifelong home on a ranch where independent spirits were exalted.

There is today a radical animal-rights movement that, at its most extreme, wants to rid the land of ranchers and stockfarmers on the theory that they exploit and callously abuse the animals in their care. Kathy Greenwood's stories give a different picture. They tell of a stockman's love for his animals, of a protectiveness that persists despite the hundred daily aggravations that are his lot. The fact that the Greenwoods know all their cattle individually, and even have named many of them, indicates the devotion they feel for their charges.

The truth, despite much nonsensical propaganda to the contrary, is that most ranchers and farmers take good care of their livestock. In the first place, it would be financially ruinous not to, for the animals represent a sizable investment. They are the factory that produces a livelihood for their owners, a factory that would collapse if not humanely treated and maintained. But beyond purely economic considerations, most livestock operators—especially those born into the trade—have a genuine affection for their animals. It is one of the reasons they remain in an occupation that year in and year out is physically demanding and offers a relatively poor financial return for the investment. In short, most people in it remain because they enjoy it as a way of life well enough to put up with its being a hard way to make a living.

It is easy to see that the Greenwoods enjoy the life and that they love their land. The hurt and sense of loss when the government takes away four sections for a dam project goes beyond purely economic concern for the ranch's ability to continue to provide a living. Giving up a piece of land on which one has lived and worked is like suffering a death in the family.

Finally, Kathy Greenwood tells about facing a dilemma that comes to most youths raised on a ranch or farm: how to deal with the parting. Only a small percentage can remain on the land. Economics dictate that most find another way to make a living, perhaps far away and certainly under a different lifestyle than they have known. Once they have done so, many find themselves caught between two worlds, feeling completely at home in neither. There is a disquieting sense of having become a perennial misfit, unable to return to the grassroots of their youth, yet unable to cut loose entirely and adapt to an impersonal urban environment of cement and steel, of timeclocks and deadlines and rush-hour traffic.

Mention of western ranches usually brings to mind the giants—the King Ranch, the 6666, the Pitchfork, or the Waggoner. But the fact is that most cattle are raised on small and medium-sized operations where the owner and his family do most of the work, aided on special occasions by trade-out neighbor help and by friends from town who want to be cowboys for a day.

This book tells about life on one of these smaller ranches, even though twenty sections—not quite thirteen thousand acres—would look huge to someone who knows only the narrow confines of the city. A ranch's size is determined by the number of livestock it can graze, not by how long the ride is from one side of it to the other. In the Greenwoods' part of New Mexico, where rain comes infrequently and without predictability, it takes more than sixty acres to keep a cow.

But small ranch or large, many of the traditions and

the working patterns are the same. The author's stories about her father and mother in many ways reflect my own experience. Hart Greenwood seems like Buck Kelton all over again. As a youngster, Kathy was frustrated by her father's never explaining anything but expecting her to know what to do. My father, a ranch foreman, almost never explained his methods or his reasons. I was expected simply to know them, or to pick them up by observation and intuition. My lack of intuitive powers kept me in trouble or under ridicule much of the time.

Yet, she shows her father's thoughtful and sympathetic nature in such incidents as his reluctance to hurt the feelings of an inept townsman by sending Kathy out to correct the fellow's error without the townsman knowing about it. At the same time, he was indirectly letting her know she had "made a hand" and was worthy of his confidence, something he would never tell her in so many words.

At roundup time, my father often was in charge of twelve to fifteen cowboys, but he did not give direct orders. It was always "If it's all right with you, I'd appreciate it if you'd . . ." or "Would you mind droppin' off here and workin' down through that draw?"

He never met Hart Greenwood, but they thought alike. I've met Hart Greenwood just once, at a ranchers' gathering in Roswell, but after reading his daughter's book, I feel that I've known him, and life on the Heart-Diamond, all my life.

In a sense, I suppose I have.

Elmer Kelton
San Angelo, Texas

1   *Heart-Diamond*

THE HEART-DIAMOND, the ranch on which I grew up, is called the Heart-Diamond for the logical reason that my father's brand is a ♥̇, and that is because his name is Hart and my grandfather, Hart Sr., had already appropriated the simple ♡ brand. Choosing to modify the basic pattern by adding a diamond had little to do with any youthful optimism on my father's part that his ranching career would be more lustrous than his father's had been, and much to do with the practical advantages of being able to form a ◇ quickly by turning the ♡-shaped "stamp iron" upside down, once the animal has been branded with it, and touching only its pointed tip (∧) to the hide in the proper place. It is useful to be able to create all the parts of each brand and all the brands the ranch needs with a single stamp iron, for otherwise it is possible to have too many irons in the fire.

When I came along and then my sister and my brother, certain ornaments and arabesques had to be tacked on. Our brands could not always be made with a single iron, but they all included some kind of heart. The theory behind this was that the neighbors, into whose pastures some of our cows invariably strayed and who generally had better things to keep track of than the brands of all their neighbors' kids, would know that a heart of any kind belonged to the Heart-Diamond. As luck would have it, however, the only other person in the state of New Mexico licensed to brand a variation on the heart lived on a ranch across the Pecos River from ours, and his strays were almost always returned to our pastures by mistake. Nonetheless, our brands worked out well even if they did not all share the logic and simplicity of my grandfather's pure heart.

The most important features of the Heart-Diamond cannot be located on maps, of course, but reside in the memories and imaginations of its inhabitants. Nevertheless, it occupies a physical space in southeastern New Mexico between Carlsbad, home of the famous Carlsbad Caverns, a tourist attraction vital to the area's economy, and Artesia, home of the less famous but equally vital Bennie's Western Wear, purveyor of hats, boots, and jeans to the local ranchers, farmers, and cowboys. The Heart-Diamond is, therefore, in the southeastern quadrant of the desert Southwest, that immense region in which cows were first introduced to this country. The Spanish explorers who marched up from Mexico in the early 1500s to find and plunder the seven cities of gold brought cows with them to eat along the way in much the same fashion that nowadays we pack a dozen steakfingers to munch on at the Fourth of July picnic. It took the Spanish a century to figure out there were no gold cities—not even one—and to abandon their search. It seems the Pueblo Indians built their cities out of adobe instead of gold, perversely maintaining that adobe was easier to come by and more comfortable to live in than gold, for which heresy many were slaughtered or sold into slavery.

But surely it took the Spaniards less time to abandon their cattle, who, if they were anything like their descendants, did not particularly relish long hikes and vented their dissatisfaction in ways that gradually eroded whatever patience the explorers might have set out with. The members of these parties of intrepid adventurers who were too tired to walk back to Mexico or too sore to ride back, settled down in adobe houses of their own. Their children and their children's children, ignoring the wisdom of the ancients (as is the custom and privilege of children), began after awhile to take a new interest in the cows, now grown wild, as did other peoples who trickled into the region. To these newcomers, the tough-hided, long-horned, mean-tempered, but marginally edible critter was at first a novelty. Then somebody got the idea to mass market cows—to sell them for food (maybe Easterners would buy them if nobody else would)—and to make a fortune. Out of the misguided notion that it probably "wouldn't hurt at least to *try*" to make a living by selling longhorns sprang the rancher, who has had more than a century of experience with cattle but who has so far not relearned what the Spanish figured out long ago.

By western standards, the Heart-Diamond is a small ranch—approximately twenty sections or about 12,800 acres. That's not too many considering that there are 121,336 sections in New Mexico and that, according to the Bureau of Land Management at least, one cow requires approximately sixty-four acres of grazing space per year. A quick calculation will reveal that the Heart-Diamond constitutes one–six thousand sixty-sixth of New Mexico and runs about two hundred cows. It is obviously not one of those giant cattle kingdoms carved out of the wilderness (although it may begin to feel like one if you spend a day riding any of its three largest pastures). In fact, my parents bought it when they were very young from a dentist, who probably foresaw what an impossible financial cavity to fill it would eventually become. He loved it nevertheless, and sold it only because the "right" people came along.

Furthermore, it is a sliver, not a carving, being much longer than it is wide. One of its borders is the famous Pecos River, west of which there was, according to the history books, a general dearth of law and order during the settling of the frontier. Fortunately, the Heart-Diamond, though it happens to be nearer the Pacific than the notorious town of Pecos, Texas (for example), falls on the eastern, more civilized bank of the river, and its residents have always been gentle, mostly law-abiding souls, shielded from the brutalizing influences of the woolly west by the Pecos' satiny (if somewhat alkaline) currents. The Atchison, Topeka, and Santa Fe Railroad kindly furnishes the ranch's eastern boundary, a track whipping across the hills like a neat stitch, and kindly runs over (and thus obviates the need to fetch home) those cows who crawl through the poorly maintained fences enclosing the tracks. The river, for all the rough-and-tumble reputation it shares with the town named after it, does not mete out such harsh punishment to trespassers now that dams have tamed its once-mighty waters. Rather, it benignly allows cows to ford its shallow channel in their quest for the grass in the neighbor's pasture, which is, of course, greener than their own. It feeds two man-made lakes, one located at each end of the ranch. The northern one, MacMillan, is large and deep enough to attract hundreds of weekend fishermen and boaters; the southern one, Avalon, is close enough to Carlsbad to attract hundreds of weekend lovers and midnight revelers, some of whom recently burned down the last of the huge cottonwood trees growing on the lake front, thus effectively destroying the scenic spot that had enticed them there in the first place.

The Heart-Diamond is bounded on three sides by water; nonetheless, its landscape is typical Southwest—or rather, since the Southwest offers an impressively wide assortment of topographies, its landscape is typical southeastern Southwest. Obviously, it is in the Pecos River Valley, which lies below and to the east of the Guadalupe Mountains, whose reeflike contours are clearly visible from my parents' house. The terrain of the ranch itself includes gently rolling, somewhat rocky hills; wide, shallow, brush-and-grass–filled draws that carry water to the river during heavy rains; open expanses of flatland covered with tabosa grass; and lakey or low places, also thick with brush and grass and pocked with sinkholes and the burrows of various small animals. The climate is, of course, arid. It is extremely hot in the summer and frequently cold in the winter, but rarely viciously or prolongedly so.

Although it is desert, the Heart-Diamond, fortunately for its grazing herds, is not barren sand. Rather, like most of the rest of the Southwest, it is home to a variety of hearty plants, bushes, and grasses, as well as to an occasional tree.

Chief among its vegetation, of course, is the cactus. The most widely represented of this fascinating species of plant are the yucca or Spanish dagger, the prickly pear, and a small, dome-shaped, needle-encased devil called *manca caballo* or "horse crippler" for its habit of lurking unseen in the shadows of bushes or rocks and then leaping suddenly into the path of an oncoming foot or hoof. Despite its antisocial behavior, however, the *manca caballo*, like other cacti, is strangely beautiful. The velvet sheen of its green surface invites the touch at the same time that a forest of needles forbids it. Like the other cacti, it blooms in late spring, putting forth waxy, fist-sized flowers that splash the hills with gaudy colors.

The yucca, a large bundle of stiletto-shaped leaves, sends up a six-foot-high, bare stalk at the top of which sprouts such a profusion of stiff, cream-colored blossoms that the stalk bends beneath their weight and the whole plant appears to be on the verge of toppling over. Cows, who crave yucca blooms, may often be found loitering near particularly rich clusters of them, presumably on the off chance that the plant will, indeed, fall or that a more enterprising cow—one who has learned to rear up on the flimsy stalk and break it off—will appear on the scene. While this latter hope may not be entirely misplaced, the assumption that another cow will cheerfully share the fruits of her labors surely is.

The prickly pear varies in size from window plant to hedge bush and features stiff, tear-shaped "leaves" bristling with thorns. It produces a red "pear" about the size of a fifty-cent piece, which may, at the expense of a few bloody fingers, be picked, peeled (the pear is covered with fine stickers), and either eaten on the spot or made into jelly. During droughts, cows may learn to eat not only the fruit but the meaty, succulent leaves of the prickly pear as well, bravely biting them off and sweeping them along the ground to remove the thorns. A pear-eater always looks as though she's on the outs with the resident porcupine.

Countless other less eye-catching though hardly less skin-piercing plants and bushes thrive in the desert, the most ubiquitous being the mesquite bush. Its delicate fern-shaped leaf conceals not-so-delicate inch-long thorns. The mesquite fruit, however, a bean rich in sugar, is easy to pluck, even for tender-nosed horses, who stuff themselves with the goody and then have to be treated for prodigious stomach aches.

Mesquite generally grows in sprawling thickets along the bottoms of draws and lakey places. It is a food source, a shade tree, a back-scratcher, and a hiding place all rolled into one as far as cows are concerned. As far as the southwestern cowboy is concerned, it is the necessity that mothered the invention of chaps. It grows about thigh high, if the thigh belongs to the rider of a typically sized cowhorse, and it is a key component in most roundups. Cows melt into mesquite thickets the moment a cowboy appears, and cowboys spend most of their day digging cows back out of them. Without mesquite, clearly, many hands would be out of work.

Lured into a stand of mesquite by an uncooperative cow, the cowboy may encounter all manner of wildlife besides his quarry. Coyotes, rattlesnakes, rabbits, lizards, horned toads, porcupines, drylanders (a kind of tortoise), owls, scorpions, skunks, badgers, raccoons, roadrunners, foxes, deer, tarantulas, quail, dove, ground squirrels, and sundry other desert dwellers seek the comfort and protection provided by the mesquite. This is not to say that a brushy draw is always teeming with animal life, only that the cowboy will not be surprised to encounter one or another of these creatures perched on a branch or sprawled in the shade of the roots of some particularly inviting bush, enduring the long afternoon and probably feeling too hot and lazy to do much more than glare at an intruder.

Another common and prickly resident of the draws and lakey places is the catclaw, a bush whose thorns, as might be surmised from its name, resemble the claws of a peevish house cat—short, curved, and likely to strike without provocation or warning. Unlike the cat, however, who courteously removes his weapons from the flesh once he has delivered his petulant blow, catclaw leaves behind poison-tipped thorns. The wound must swell and fester before the thorn can be removed.

The crown-of-thorns bush is much rarer (and more threatening) than either mesquite or catclaw. Its branches wield three-inch-long spikes, which are said to have been the material out of which Jesus' tormenting crown was woven. Like a hippopotamus or a duckbilled platypus, the crown-of-thorns looks prehistoric, as though it should have disappeared from the face of the earth long ago. Cows are glad it did not, however, for they find its formidable branches useful in terrorizing the flies and other insects that reside on their hairy backs just out of reach of their tails.

All the Heart-Diamond plants are necessarily tough, as are desert plants in general, but not all are armed and dangerous. Greasewood, for example, which is found all over the hills and flats, is as unprepossessing in appearance as in name. It is, however, the perfume of the desert, releasing into the air (especially after a spring shower) a clean fragrance akin to but sweeter and subtler than the smell of pine. In addition, it is indispensable to the rider who needs, for whatever reason, to dismount in the middle of the pasture and tether his horse. Not only are its pliant branches too strong for the horse to break, they are inedible, so he is not tempted to gnaw his way to freedom.

Sagebrush grows among (and mingles its scent with) the greasewood and touches up the spring landscape with soft brushstrokes of purple. Tumbleweeds, though neither beautiful, odoriferous, nor useful, earn their keep by creating excitement and entertainment. Along with whirlwinds, with which they frequently act in concert, tumbleweeds are the pranksters of the desert. They do, indeed, tumble, once they have been uprooted by a scalding summer wind, piling up against (and sometimes overturning) fences, playing "chicken" with motorists, and scaring the wits out of sleepy horses. Honeysuckle, broomweed, jimson weed, trompillos, mustard seed, tansy, goldenrod—countless weeds, in fact—and such grasses as grama, salt, bermuda, tabosa, needle, and burro flourish in the desert soil, providing food for an assortment of animals (including the livestock of the Heart-Diamond) as well as beauty for anyone who cares to notice.

"Green" in the desert Southwest means light, lime green—a five-o'clock shadow of green—rather than the brighter luxuriance of wetter regions, and few species of plants grow taller than the average backyard fence. Existence here, nevertheless, is neither tenuous nor marginal. If it is not profligate, launching shoots and tendrils to compete for every inch of dark, damp earth, neither is it reticent nor spare. It may perch daringly on a rocky outcropping, drill far below the parched surface of a plain to find water, or enterprisingly wedge itself into the narrow strip of soil between two large boulders. It is neither wasteful nor greedy. It accepts and makes use of what is given—a sudden summer shower, a cooling breeze, a dazzling white sun—and waits stoically for what it needs.

Still, although a desert cactus is surely as lovely, in its offish way, as autumn foliage in Maine, the beauty and mystique of the Heart-Diamond and the Southwest in general reside not so much in the collective impression inspired by the vegetation as in the panoramic vistas afforded by the comparative lack of vegetation. Space, light, and curious, sometimes bizarre shapes of the terrain, as well as the interplay among these properties, create the awesome scenery of this vast stage—a scenery that both reduces the acts performed upon it and makes them plainly visible to any audience within a hundred-mile radius. The maddened darting of a cowboy trying to regather his spilled herd is a comic interlude in the morning's work to another cowboy who crests a hill on the opposite side of the pasture. Two rangy coyotes stalk a cottontail in a draw, oblivious of the horseman who sits on the ridge above watching them. A dark speck slowly assumes the shape of a cow meandering along a trail to a windmill.

A plain in the Southwest may stretch beyond the curvature of the earth, an infinite dry sea of sand, brush, and yellow-tasseled grass. Or its vast emptiness might be stunningly interrupted by a solitary jagged peak, a row of flat-topped mesas, or an enigmatic column of sandstone. Unreckonable miles away, an irregular bank of gunmetal blue mountains meets the azure sky.

At dawn, the sun bobs up behind the windmill tower that stands at a distance, tinting the sky just sufficiently to bring out the black lines of the scaffolding. The wheel starts in playful motion, quickened by a springing breeze. Gradually, as the sun penetrates the thin wall of the night's chill, the animals, too, begin to stir. Awash in the morning light, the hills seem closer than they are. At noon, all the crisp lines are blurred by waves of heat rising out of the ground, but later they reemerge, so that each physical object appears in its perfect form. A black curtain of rain may hang in the air or move slowly across the horizon, taunting the desert with the smell of water. At dusk, when humans and animals shake off their afternoon torpor and busy themselves once more, the darkening sky is rent by immense shafts of light. And at sunset . . .

Standing in the yard whose grass my parents must constantly rescue from drought, weeds, and horses, one has an unimpeded view of this legendary and spectacular finale, which is everything it's cracked up to be. It takes place at the back of the High Lonesome Pasture, or perhaps just the other side of the Guadalupes. It is difficult to tell from what spot the lights and colors stream, they illuminate so much of the sky. The brilliant glow of sunset does to the mountains what sunrise does to the windmill, vividly outlining each detail. Then gradually the peaks and valleys dissolve and merge into a single black cutout.

If any stray clouds happen to be in the vicinity, they burn angry red and molten gold for awhile and are reduced at last to ashy blue slate, cold and dull. The white glow that envelops the sun in the afternoon is quenched, and the sun itself, a perfect orange globe, plunges out of sight. The trail of light in its wake softens to a gentle iridescence, fades, and gives way to the first planet. Soon, stars saturate the sky, gleaming icily an arm's length away. The breeze carries the scent of greasewood and rustles wisps of hay. A horse noses out the last few oats in his trough and sneezes, unimpressed with the display about which less taciturn natures feel obliged to wax poetic. Crickets chirp. A coyote howls plaintively. A fence post, seen a million times during the day, loses its familiar features in the dark and gives the fleeting impression that a threatening figure may be lurking "out there," but the tiny light in the living room window beckons reassuringly. Somewhere in the pasture, a cow bawls, calling her wayward calf to her side. Time to go in.

2 *Chores*

WHEN MY FATHER milked Buttermilk, the stream hit the bottom of the pail with a tinny "ping" that the milk, as it rose, muffled to a throaty "pwish." The mounting head of foam would soon spill over the rim of the pail, and in the coolness of early morning, it smoked like the nostrils of the feeding cow. When they heard the milking begin, six or seven barn cats would arrange themselves around Buttermilk's back feet and watch expectantly for a squirt to come their way, for after squeezing three streams into the pail, my father would always aim the fourth at one or another of them. Three squeezes into the pail, squirt at cat number one; three squeezes into the pail, squirt at cat number two; three squeezes into the pail, squirt at cat number three, and so on down the line until each cat was licking milk from its jowls and forehead, anticipating the warm bowlful (actually, the cats' bowl was a discarded hubcap) for which their facial ablutions were an appetite-whetting hors d'oeuvre. The dog, just outside the gate of the pen, where he was ordered to stay lest he bark at the cow and cause a commotion, would feign utter contempt for cows, milk, and the special privileges of cats, lounging about carelessly until his portion got poured into his old frying pan, whereupon he would drop his pose and gulp voraciously. Dewdrop or Flower or Stubby or Elmo—whatever calf Buttermilk had at the time—would low urgently to be reunited with its mother and permitted to finish what had been left in her prodigiously large bag.

When my father milked the cow, the scene was pastoral, and all creatures looked forward with great relish to the first long draught of the steaming liquid that would break their night's fast.

All creatures, that is to say, except the Heart-Diamond kids, who could not stand the stuff, steaming or otherwise. Every morning we clamored for pasteurized, homogenized, or as we called it, "store-bought" milk—the kind from which the globs of cream, always to be discovered floating on the surface of a glass of Buttermilk's milk no matter how much my mother skimmed and stirred it, had been miraculously removed. My brother and sister and I all hated fresh milk, for we were then at the age when children's most passionate convictions have to do with the tastes and textures of the foods their parents force upon them. Cream globs made us gag. Even when my mother added Hershey's chocolate syrup to our milk (to disguise its sour smell on those mornings after Buttermilk had escaped from her pen and spent the night feasting on wild gourd vines), we loathed it. My mother's lecture about the folks in town who'd give anything for fresh milk were countered with the logic children typically bring to bear on such lectures. My sister, for example, suggested on one occasion when she felt particularly hemmed in that we haul Buttermilk to town in the stock trailer and dump her out. My five-year-old brother was vaguely fond of the cow and began to cry as he imagined her forlornly wandering the streets of Carlsbad. Nevertheless, he refused to drink the tall glass of milk my sister shoved at him.

Shortly after this incident, my mother gave in. She said it was silly for her to cool the milk, skim it, pour it into glasses, set it on the table, fight with us about drinking it, and *then* feed it to the cats and the dog. She said she might as well just feed it directly to them while it was still warm. After all, *they* had sense enough to like it that way. She'd buy us milk whenever she went to town, though she hoped none of the neighbors caught her doing it. She just might have to tell them how silly her kids were about drinking fresh milk, and wouldn't *we* be embarrassed? We told her to duck behind the bread counter if she saw anybody she knew. We didn't really care much what the neighbors thought, but we figured she'd be scandalized if we said so. Besides, the odds were against her running into any neighbors. We only had two, and one of them shopped in Artesia. We soothed and advised her as best we could, while secretly rejoicing that we'd worn her down at last.

As it turned out, I had further cause to celebrate our victory, for it resulted in my father deciding I should learn to milk the cow. Feeding the pets and providing my mother with a little cooking cream wouldn't require all that much milk, and he was pretty sure I could extract as much as we'd need. He had plenty of other chores and would gladly be rid of this one.

I couldn't understand my father's willingness to forego the milking. I had always wanted to learn to do it, for it seemed an important and interesting job. I accepted his proposal quickly before he had time to think about it and change his mind. I also stuck my tongue out at my brother and sister when they ridiculed the idea. They were envious, of course, for as mere children, they'd still have to do such menial chores as pick up the mysteriously proliferous baling wire and tow sacks that were always strewn around the barn floor. I assured my father that he needn't waste his valuable time teaching me, that I had watched him milk a million times and knew all about it, and that I'd start the very next day. He smiled at my mother and seemed amused, but I couldn't think why.

The next morning found me regretting slightly my cavalier dismissal of my father. It struck me that, though I knew a few things about milking, I didn't know a few others. I had always wandered out of the house in a sleepy daze about the time he was sitting down at Buttermilk's right flank, the pail wedged firmly between his knees and the cow crunching "cake" (hard cubes of pressed hay, grain, and molasses). Not confined in a stanchion, Buttermilk would stand still to be milked only so long as there was cake in her trough. This I knew. But I did not know the steps preliminary to the actual feeding and milking of the cow, briefly outlined by my father as he headed around the corner of the barn. I needed to turn the calf in to suck for a few minutes so the cow would let her milk down, he told me. Then I needed to "kick" the calf off for the several minutes it would take me to complete the task.

Likewise, I knew that Doyle, Buttermilk's current calf, who by now weighed about two hundred pounds and was no longer "Precious" (my mother's nickname for all new calves) or "Doodle Bug" (my father's), would have been separated from his mother all night to ensure an adequate milk supply. I did not know (yet) how much he resented having his breakfast interrupted so shortly after he had begun it.

The rest of the drill, however, I had down pat. You fed the cow her cake, positioned yourself on the upside-down feed bucket that served as a milking stool, grasped the milk pail with your knees, seized a left teat with your left hand and a right one with your right hand, and squeezed (left, right; left, right; left, right) until you had enough milk. Next, you let the calf back in to finish off the contents of the bag and spend the day eating hay with his mother, slopped some milk into the cats' hubcap and the dog's frying pan, and then swaggered to the house with half a pail or so for the pleased cook. Finally, you brushed off your britches before you entered the kitchen to bask in the grudging admiration of your siblings and to wash down your pancakes and bacon with a nice glass of store-bought milk.

Turning the calf in wasn't too difficult. He was hovering by the gate, waiting to hurl himself through the merest crack. He knew the drill too, of course. On the first morning, however, I committed the strategic error of feeding Buttermilk before I let Doyle in, and by the time I had fooled around reclosing the gate between her pen and his and had ordered the dog to lie down (he sized me up and then sat), her cake, to my astonishment, had disappeared. She lowered her head and waggled her dainty horns when I approached, which was as much as to say "you know the deal. Keep your hands to yourself." I now remembered my father remarking once that Buttermilk could consume ten cubes to any other cow's one, since in her determination to get as many as possible, she didn't bother chewing them but swallowed them whole. She belched them up later, he supposed, at cud-chewing time, and re-ate them in more leisurely fashion.

The implications such gluttony held for a person trying to milk Buttermilk had never really occurred to me until now, but even now I decided she could not possibly have siphoned up a gallon and a half of cake. I figured I had mismeasured the ration and returned to the barn for another one, my father's frequent admonitions against wasting expensive feed nudging the edges of my consciousness, where I kept all such admonitions. I scooped double handfuls of the cubes out of a tow sack until my feed bucket was full and trotted back to the pen. But this time, instead of pouring the entire bucketful immediately into the trough, I decided to throw in only a few cubes as a sop to Buttermilk while I put Doyle back into his pen, and to save the rest until I was ready to milk. If not a fast milker, I was at least a fast learner.

Doyle was starting on the second teat by now, his tail wagging in rhythm with the nursing reflex of his tongue and jaws, but since he was permitted the contents of two teats every morning anyway, my first mistake had resulted in little serious damage. Buttermilk had stopped snuffing her empty trough and stood, at the moment, five or six feet away from it, determined to protect the rights of her nursing infant. However, I suspected that any contest between her maternal instinct and her appetitive one would be no contest at all. My sly plan was to toss ten or twelve cake cubes into the trough. Then, at the instant Buttermilk, in dashing for them, jerked the teat out of the startled Doyle's mouth, I would step between mother and son and drive the latter back into his pen before he recovered from his confusion. I tossed and the cow dashed, but Doyle, seemingly accustomed to arbitrary fits and starts of the bag, hung on for dear life. The violence of his mother's lunge swung his body in an arc that left it perpendicular to hers, but he continued to suck, sidling rapidly like a crab to keep up with her.

But at least now that she was preoccupied with eating cake, Buttermilk would let me walk up to her and do whatever I wanted to do with Doyle. She more or less ignored me when I placed my left hand flat on her hip to brace myself while, with my right, I tried to pry loose the nursing calf. I pushed hard on her flank for leverage and pulled mightily on his nose, and finally, with a wet plop, his mouth lost its hold, and he came up for air, slobbering and blowing milk bubbles. I quickly wedged my entire body between his thrusting head and Buttermilk's belly, but Doyle was prepared for such a maneuver and spun a circle on his hind legs, racing under his mother's neck to get at the bag from the other side. He had drunk three-fourths of the third teat by the time I got him loose again. And, of course, Buttermilk was out of cake by now, which meant that she was no longer a neutral power in the war between Doyle and me. She threw all her weight (and it was not inconsiderable) into his corner, moving her body in such a way that, no matter which direction I shoved or pulled Doyle's head, she managed to keep her bag at the tip of his tongue. His head was attracted to that bag like a magnet to metal. I restrained the impulse to brain both Doyle and Buttermilk with a cedar post that had fallen out of the fence, and headed instead for the cake bucket.

On the way there, I conceived another plan for outwitting this cow, who so far had been milking *me* for all *I* was worth. Concealing my new scheme behind a poker face, I chased both Doyle and his mother into Doyle's pen and slammed the gate. Then I poured my remaining cubes into Buttermilk's trough while she eyed me through the fence, the wheels of her bovine brain spinning faster as she pondered this apparent hitch in what had otherwise been a bang-up morning for her. My intention was to persuade Buttermilk to get rid of Doyle herself. The perfect world for her was one in which she got all the cake and Doyle got all the milk, but forced to choose between the two imperfect alternatives—the one in which Doyle could guzzle but she couldn't, or the one in which she waxed fat while he pined and wasted—she'd sacrifice Doyle every time. All I had to do was make her understand that the ideal was not possible and that only cooperation with me could bring about the better of the other two options. I opened the gate just a hint, pretending I might let her back into the pen where the heap of cubes was glistening in the morning light. But when she poked a tentative nose through the opening, I lightly thumped it and then banged the gate sharply in her face.

Buttermilk was nobody's fool. She knew from my father's having milked her for three years that Doyle was supposed to be separated from her by now, and she rapidly deduced that only by abandoning him would she be allowed to feed her face again. Doyle's fate was sealed. Turning abruptly from the gate, Buttermilk trotted a wide circle around the pen, testing the strength of Doyle's hold on her teat. He sidestepped as before, glugging down what little milk remained in her bag. Then, having calculated the degree of surprise and force necessary to "unplug" the calf, Buttermilk suddenly launched her round-paunched, red-orange self into a run, the speed of which I would not have thought her capable. Doyle was as shocked by it as I was apparently, for he was left behind in a cloud of dust, bloated and burping. Buttermilk completed her second turn around the pen and dove for the gate, which I opened just enough to clear her huge girth before closing it once again, this time in Doyle's smeary face.

Hearing the staccato rap of teeth on cake—with a karate chop of the jaws, Buttermilk appeared to be breaking each of the three-inch-long cubes in half before swallowing it—I worked hurriedly to spot my milk stool at her flank, to seat myself on it, to grip the pail with my knees, and to grab a teat in each hand. I was ready to go at last. The cats, who had begun to pace nervously, looked relieved as they formed a semicircle around Buttermilk's back end.

But when I squeezed the left teat, nothing happened. It was warm and dry and kind of stretchy like the fingers of a dish-washing glove or the skin of a snake. I squeezed the right one, gluey from Doyle's mouth, and a barely visible spider's thread of milk spattered the knee of my Levis. It was unpleasantly hot and sticky. "You gotta be careful where ya aim these things, I guess," I said with forced gaiety to no cat in particular. A gray female crept up to lick my Levis but leaped away when the milk pail, submitted to too much pressure by my nervous knees, shot under Buttermilk's belly and landed with a clatter. As I stood to retrieve it, I noticed an ominous silence and, without bothering to glance into the trough, trudged resignedly toward the barn for more cake. Buttermilk nodded sweetly as the third bucket of shiny cubes tumbled around her nose. I sat down on my stool again.

This time, I placed the milk pail on the ground directly below the teats (it was too big around for me to hold between my knees, I decided), hoping to enlist the aid of gravity and to make the angle of my shot less severe. I squeezed the left teat, but it fired blanks again. To bring more of my arm muscles into play, I moved my stool four or five inches further away from Buttermilk's bag and then tilted forward on it, resting my forehead against her flank to keep from toppling over. She flinched when I touched this ticklish part of her anatomy but didn't otherwise move. The cats were beginning to get restless again, and the dog was asleep. Grimly determined, I gave the left teat a tremendous squeeze and simultaneously pulled down on it; all the weight of my body leaned to the effort. My forehead gouged Buttermilk, and so now she did move, of course, causing me to fall off my stool and the cats to scatter. But lo and behold, two pearly beads of milk appeared at the end of the teat, and, though both dropped into the dust by Buttermilk's hooves, more came out when I recovered and plied my new technique. Buttermilk stood firm, not seeming to mind the pawing and pinching. Her flank, in which I had buried my nose as well as my forehead, was soft, and she smelled, I noticed, better than the dog usually did. Soon, I had about a sixteenth of an inch of liquid in my pail, and the cats looked reinspired. To reward and encourage their patience, I aimed a squirt at a loudmouthed, black-and-white tom, but when the milk came out in a fine-spun trickle and landed a foot in front of him, I decided to stick to the basics.

In a few minutes, the ground beneath Buttermilk's bag was soggy, but the sixteenth inch had doubled to an eighth inch, and I had begun to get the hang of milking. Admittedly, most of what my pail held had come from the easier right teat, the one Doyle had primed, not from the left one, which he had not yet tapped. Instead of the two ropey strands my father's strong hands drew out, mine managed only three drops and a shimmery thread, three drops and a shimmery thread, three drops and a shimmery thread. Nevertheless, this was progress, even if the cats *had* meandered off one by one to check out the mouse population in the haybarn. At least the dog was sitting up again. "Now we're cookin'," I said to myself as I squeezed and tugged. I discovered that if, before I squeezed, I pushed the teat a little way up into the bag, the milk would flow down into it and could then be stripped out, much as you strip the toothpaste out of its tube when for some reason you want all of it at once. The sun had finally cleared the hill behind our house and beamed mildly on my back and on my labors.

The next thing I knew, Buttermilk had plopped her right hind foot in the middle of my pail. The black dirt that washed off her hoof transformed my eighth inch of foam into a lavalike goo. The back end of the factory having absorbed all my attention, I had neglected to monitor the front end, whose various dials and gauges would have given me fair warning that milking operations were about to shut down unless somebody stoked the furnace. I stood up, keeping my legs stiff so my wet Levis wouldn't touch them, and glared at Buttermilk, who informed me via a careless toss of her head that she didn't give a hoot about my glare, that I could glare all day or for the rest of my life if I wanted to, that, glare or no glare, there'd be no more milking until there was more cake.

I began to understand the phrase "to be on the horns of a dilemma." I did not want to suffer the humiliation of having exchanged seven or eight buckets of cake for a cupful of slime, nor did I relish having to explain the disappearance of all that feed to my father, nor, above all, did

I wish to endure the breakfast-table gibes of my brother and sister. Escape plans began to parade themselves through my imagination, but each seemed fatally flawed. I did not, for example, know how to shift the pickup out of first gear, in which it traveled much more slowly than most people (even my parents) could run; I did not know precisely where Timbuktoo was, though I had gathered from an expression of my mother's that it was comfortably distant from my present location; nor was I certain the army would accept a woman my age.

Dismissing these, which I knew were the outlandish in my crowd of ideas, I considered the more conservative ones—lying or faking a life-threatening illness—but saw problems in them too. I was a terrible liar, whose eyes shifted guiltily and whose nose grew at an alarming rate, and if I were to develop an illness, I'd have to spend the rest of the day in bed and eat milk-toast—fresh milk-toast, in all likelihood, since my mother hadn't been to town yet.

Time was running out. I could smell bacon cooking (was it mine?), and my stomach growled hungrily. Soon, my father, having finished his own chores, would come to check on my progress. He'd ask a lot of embarrassing questions and might even decide, meaning to be kind, that I wasn't old enough yet to butt heads with Buttermilk. The nuances of feeling and understanding I shared with my father that would make demotion at his hands bearable did not register, I believed, in the puerile souls of my brother and sister, so I might just as well be marched to the center of the parade grounds and have my shiny new bars ripped off my uniform. But my brain had not given up, and as it rifled through its now-scanty collection of options, it discovered a new one—telling the truth, at which, at first, it merely laughed, but toward which it gradually warmed.

I let Doyle back in to finish off the fourth teat. He had already drunk too much milk and would probably be scoured, but even at his early age, he showed signs of having inherited his mother's ability to eat huge quantities of food with no ill effect, so he'd probably survive (although I hoped not). I consoled myself with the thought that, even if Buttermilk had won the first skirmish, she had not yet carried the battle. She had to see my throwing in the bucket (the very one she had kicked) as a sign that I drew the line somewhere—that even though I couldn't milk worth a darn, I was nevertheless a person who did not take being trifled with sitting down. "Forget it," I told her when she looked significantly at her empty trough, "not even if you were starving."

"Fat chance," her look replied. I threw her a smaller-than-usual block of hay and dejectedly set off for the house.

Along the way, I began to consider how the truth might actually appear to my audience, and suddenly there flashed through my mind the image of a skull and crossbones, like the one I'd noticed on the box of rat poison in the cabinet. I did not understand this dire warning. Telling the truth was supposed to lead to a better life—to loyal friends, loving parents, plenty of candy—not to death. Somewhat unnerved, I decided to rehearse my lines. The truth was (everybody knew it!) that Buttermilk ate too fast. Even my father, I was now convinced, had occasionally lost the race to fill his pail before she emptied her trough, and I, a mere novice, could not be expected to prevail over her in our first encounter. "But an eighth inch of mud?"

sarcastically inquired the skull, appearing again and now sporting my sister's blond hair and my brother's mischievous green eyes. "I mean *really* fast," I replied solemnly, hoping that maybe such a tone would cut short my siblings' taunts and that the uncanniness of the speed with which Buttermilk ate cake would be more interesting to them than my failure. But I knew, deep down, that they'd stick like burrs to the topic of my empty milk pail, and I asked myself ironically if the truth was really going to get me out of this mess. Fat chance! But maybe, with a little help, it could.

It seemed to me, as I thought about it, my hand poised on the knob of the side door to the kitchen, that The Truth could best be assisted by The Facts. Instead of stretching it, embellishing it, magnifying or otherwise distorting it, I would tell it so strictly but so completely that no cracks or crevasses, through which the caustic laughter of my brother and sister might penetrate, would mar its tough surface. If the truth were that Buttermilk ate too fast for all but the most accomplished milkers (my father) to get anything like a full quota of milk, then I needed to know exactly *how* fast she ate. I set my pail down behind a rosebush (the dog sniffed it disparagingly), walked through the front door of the house into the living room, opened the top drawer of the big cabinet standing along one wall, and drew out a stop watch, which hung on a leather thong and which my mother used to time my father when he practiced roping calves before competing in the V-J Day Rodeo every year.

I went out the way I had entered so my mother wouldn't see me, and as I walked back to the pens, I played and edited several times the imaginary scene of my breakfast conversation-to-be. In one version, I allowed my brother and sister to commit themselves irretrievably, enduring their brutally sarcastic teasing before informing them (either with a triumphant laugh or with quiet significance, I couldn't decide which) that *in fact* Buttermilk had eaten X number of cubes in X minutes. A stunned silence followed this announcement, and then I finished my breakfast to the sweet tune of their amazed "oohs" and "aahs." The truth was beginning to have a better feel.

Back at the barn, I dipped another gallon of feed from the sack. Hearing the promising rattle of cubes, Buttermilk recovered from the funk into which my departure seemed to have thrown her and moved eagerly toward her trough. I was intrigued with my new plan and did not stop to consider how my return must have looked to her or what it might seem to imply about the outcome of our contest of wills. I was after the whole truth and nothing could keep me from it. I said these words out loud and wondered for a moment if this was the sort of dedication to a quest that propelled men and women into greatness. I saw myself as President and then as a swimmer saving a drowning child but perishing herself. A few proud tears blurred the numbers on the stop watch, but, getting control of myself, I grasped the watch in my left hand, my thumb poised over the starting button; with my right hand I dumped the cake into the trough. Wanting to be strictly accurate and not to falsify the outcome of my experiment, I did not click the watch until Buttermilk's long agile tongue curled around the first cube. Doyle, swollen and sick, stood sullenly in the far corner of the pen, totally uninterested in these novel proceedings.

Buttermilk was truly amazing. After thirty seconds, she had devoured what appeared to me to be roughly a quarter of a gallon of cake. At this rate, she'd be through the entire gallon in two minutes, a phenomenal speed that would assuredly impress my breakfast audience. At fifty seconds, I watched the last cube of the first half-gallon disappear (she seemed to pick up speed as she went along), and at the very moment I yelled out "sixty seconds!" in my great excitement, my father's hat, followed by his furrowed brow and quizzical eyes, appeared at the top of the milk-cow pen gate.

Talk about bad timing.

3 Cow and Bull Story

EVEN THOUGH WE HAVE A MILK COW, the Heart-Diamond is a ranch, not a dairy. Milk cows are pale, domesticated shadows of the real pasture dweller, although old-timers claim that the modern ranch cow is an effete remnant of her rangy, foul-tempered ancestor. Like people, cows have gotten soft over the years. This business about Buttermilk implies that I learned cows from the ground up through hands-on experience. But actually, I studied them mainly from the rear-end view provided by my trusty cowhorse, as he and I followed them along the hundreds of miles of narrow trails that crisscross the Heart-Diamond and link together its windmills, water holes, choice grazing spots, and pasture gates. On good days, the hollow clip-clop of his shod hooves kept time with their cushiony two-toed tread, and to this agreeably drowsy melody, all our heads bobbed in unison. On good days, we resembled a well-rehearsed dance troupe, dipping and swaying along the rocky ridges and sloping hills as we headed for the Middle Pasture windmill or the Lake Pasture gate or the Horse Pasture water hole.

On bad days, however, of which there were not a few, we were a swarm of angry insects, a straggling line of weary war refugees, or the rowdy mob at a political rally by the time we finally got where we were going. And on one particularly awful day, we didn't arrive at all. The rest of the hands and the cattle they had brought in were all congregated at the High Lonesome windmill, the hands swapping rodeo stories while their horses nosed at the water in the trough, having already drunk their fill. A fine breeze blew and the windmill turned rapidly, pumping a thin stream of water into the rock holding tank. Tired from their morning trek, the cattle sprawled around the tank or scratched themselves lazily. They were at that moment a docile bunch and not likely to try to escape, even if not closely guarded. Every now and then, one of the cowboys cast a precautionary glance their way (still listening carefully to the joke another cowboy was telling) and then looked west, from which quadrant he expected me to appear at any second. Roundup etiquette would not permit him to remain idle if he supposed I needed help, especially because I was a female. Neither, however, would it permit him to "hurry" unless he was sure a crisis was impending. Conflicting forces then, like the currents that momentarily transfix quivering fish, held my potential rescuers at the trough for a few more precious seconds.

Just as they gathered up their slackened reins, replanted their feet in their stirrups, and pulled their hats down, the hands saw galloping headlong out of the west three grey, two-year-old Brahman heifers, who obviously did not intend to stop at the windmill or even, for that matter, in the county. Several fleet horsemen managed to bend the paths of the runaways into a wide circle around the windmill, and finally, as the main herd exerted its gravitylike influence on them, two of the three slowed down and eventually stopped, bawling loudly a few times before trotting over to join their friends. The third, a sleek model raised in the Texas Panhandle, merely gathered speed and, with a final sprint, went into orbit, shooting the gap between a pair of lathered cowhorses and cursing hands. Unless the boss needed her bad enough for them to run her down and rope her, she might just as well be left alone. She was too riled to be reasonable and was last seen rocketing toward some distant planet on which cowboys and cowhorses had not yet evolved. "Reckin we'll git 'er next time," said one outmaneuvered but unperturbed rider to the other, secretly wondering what on earth I had done to upset the heifers.

For he correctly supposed that the three white heifers were cattle that I had "started." He speculated about the nature of the trouble that had befallen me and joined with the rest of the hands in anticipating the teasing that I would surely merit and that they would gladly administer. But finally, this prologue gotten through, he and the rest moseyed out to hunt for me, chuckling, spitting tobacco juice, and calculating the odds of my having fallen off my horse—a catastrophe that would greatly spice up the next several gossip sessions at the water trough.

Without actually witnessing this scene at the windmill—which I could not do because I was still a mile and a half beyond that very western horizon toward which the cowboys were now guiding their horses—I knew what it was, for I had participated in similar ones, contributing my own two-cents worth of wit to the general fund being raised on the occasion of somebody else's misfortune. I imagined the Brahman heifers delaying the hands for a little while but supposed they would also signal my need for help. I could "hear" the hands telling a few final anecdotes, interspersing them with various strategies and plans for my rescue, but I knew that at last a search would be initiated and that I would be found. I knew, and I shuddered with dread.

Don't get me wrong. Under ordinary circumstances, the sight of a grinning cowboy come to "save" me would have been a welcome one. You've never needed help until you've needed help with cattle, and no amount of teasing can diminish the gratitude you feel when you get it. But the circumstances on this particular day were not ordinary, and at precisely the instant I could "see" the three heifers plunging down the hill toward the windmill, my heart sank. I pulled to a halt my exhausted horse, who clearly agreed with the fleeing heifers that I was a menace to all life, and I tried to "get ahold" of myself. But when I looked at the cow and the bull in front of me and when I thought about six cow*boys* coming to help me drive them, I wanted to cry.

Why did this happen to me? If I had found the cow and bull earlier, perhaps the cow would not have been in heat. Or if I had found them a little later, perhaps she'd have been begging the Hereford bull for satisfaction, which would surely have been speedily supplied. Afterwards, he would have subsided for a time into a slothful tractability and she into her quotidian, businesslike routine. Right *then*, however, at that exact moment, the cow wasn't quite ready for the bull, though she didn't want to be too unfriendly—she figured she'd have some use for him later. But he, predicting that she'd soon say "yes," was not about to leave her alone, even when she turned and hooked at him. He understood the meaning of those kinds of hooks and swallowed them all, along with the line and the sinker too, as they say. She'd given him a lukewarm shoulder, and though he'd have preferred hotter temperatures and a more choice section of her anatomy, he knew she'd "come around" in a little while. Bulls and cows are such *animals* about sex! Normally, I might have found her coquetry and his brutish perseverance charming and educational, but as it was, I would have driven Juliet and her Romeo over the nearest cliff if I had thought I could get them there.

My unexpected appearance in the lakey place where the mating ritual was unfolding, and my appeal to its celebrants to join with me and the cattle I had already found and collected—the three Brahman heifers and five mama cows with their babies—in a journey to the windmill had not been sympathetically received. In fact, the cow and the bull had been so engrossed in the mysteries of love and passion that they had ignored me completely until I had yelled at them. I would have preferred leaving them alone, as they would have preferred to have been left alone, but I had orders, and orders from my father were not mere suggestions or guidelines to be implemented only if I found it convenient to do so. He wanted all the bulls in this pasture, and he wanted all the cows, and he wanted everything else too that we could find and bring in.

I knew that driving the star-struck lovers would be about as easy as visiting the stars themselves. Nevertheless, the choice between attempting the impossible and explaining to my father why I hadn't attempted it would have been simple, had it not been for the six cowboys—the six, young, male cowboys—who had been hired for this roundup, and who, when they beheld the spectacle of my flirtatious cow and lusty bull, would have to refrain totally, out of deference to me and my gender, from all open or covert jokes or comments of even a remotely sexual nature. Having looked forward all morning to finding me in some interesting dilemma, they would find me in what would be to them the most interesting dilemma of all, the kind having to do with raw sex. But they'd have to keep their mouths shut. The smarmy jokes and smirking wit that the lascivious antics of my lovers could not help but inspire would have to wait, and for the duration of the eternal ride back to the windmill, we'd all pretend that the cow and the bull were not doing what they were doing. The same etiquette that would compel the hands to come to my aid would compel them not to engage in conversation of a risqué cast with a female of twelve, especially when that female was the boss's daughter. Even more rigid was the convention that required me never to have heard of sex before, though surely anybody who stopped and thought for a minute would realize that I couldn't help but know a little about the drives and processes in the midst of which I'd lived all my life and upon which the ranch's economy was based. Nevertheless, for an endless half hour at least, naked nature would cavort and gambol before us, and we'd have to talk about how I liked the seventh grade or where I got my new saddle.

Do not misunderstand me. Although I was confident that my delicate sensibility would survive a brush with the coarse images that inevitably emerge in young men's discussions of sex, I wanted to be spared, for I did not know these young men well enough to exchange pleasantries of even a slightly personal nature, much less gross obscenities. A sophisticated woman of twelve, however, does not like to be thought naive, especially about sex, and my naiveté, as well as my current predicament, would doubtlessly be the topic of stories and jokes told behind my back when the boys gathered later at the pickups and trailers to unsaddle their horses. Even the most innocuous comment I might make to demonstrate my "savvy" ("boy, ya can't do a thing with them when they're you-know-what!") was forbidden. My self-image, in short, was at stake, and for that reason, I almost left the cow and the bull behind, orders or no orders. But somebody would ultimately have found them and would have asked me how I could have missed them, or worse, would have figured out that I had "missed" them on purpose—and why. What's the difference between hanging at the end of a short rope and hanging at the end of a long one? You're dead either way.

So I picked up the cow and the bull. It wasn't that they had been actively resisting my efforts to take them to the windmill. Their thoughts were simply elsewhere. For two hours, unless I rode at a spot two feet off the left shoulder of the distracted cow, she drifted northeast, followed ardently by the hulking bull. He did not want her out of smelling range, which was apparently, in these cases, rather restricted. The trouble was that the rest of my collection was following a trail which ran through a little draw that was a veritable garden of fresh green sproutlets and spriglets of grass. They couldn't pass up a single mouthful, and unless I dogged their heels every step of the way, shouting and whooping, they stopped to graze. And so I made endless forays between them, as they meandered along the bottom of the draw, and the cow and the bull, who, obeying some mandate of a realm that only they inhabited, found it necessary to walk at a much more rapid pace and in the wrong direction along the tops of the rises on the north side of the draw.

I probably would have gotten us all to the windmill and averted the humiliation about to be visited upon me if the powers that assumed command of the cow each time I abandoned my post by her side to gallop back down to the other cows had not abruptly turned her completely around. Up to that point, her course had resembled a series of giant rainbows laid end to end, the apogee of each being the spot at which my horse and I had appeared suddenly in her peripheral vision and startled her back into an easterly direction. This meant that a certain percentage of the time (albeit a small one), the cow and the bull had been headed toward the windmill. By dint of much aggressive shouting, running, and turning, I figured I could top the hill overlooking it just as the punch line to the last Artesia rodeo "reride" story induced the requisite guffaws in the crew at the water trough.

But naturally, just as I was beginning to take comfort in this thought, the cow stopped dead in her tracks, turned and stared at the bull (who had bumped into her), and then began to walk northwest. Who knows why? I yanked at my bridle reins as the oblivious pair began to retrace the ground we had just traversed at such great emotional and physical expense on my part. Tender of mouth and agile of foot, my horse spun so lightly on his hind legs and so catlike that he nearly unseated me. He knew his job and resented my harsh hand. Somewhere beneath the rage that was beginning to uncurl in my chest, I was ashamed of myself and patted his neck. He made no sign that he forgave me.

We circled around the cow and the bull, who, as it

turned out, had no serious commitment to the northwest and did not resist when I turned them back toward the draw. They were two tumbleweeds being blown about by the same whirlwind, mindless, for all that they appeared to be engaged in a perfectly synchronized ballet. I urged them into a brisk trot because the rest of the bunch had finally quickened their pace. Having caught the scent of water in the breeze that stirred the greasewood and mesquite bushes, they would maintain a steady walk straight to the windmill. My anger retreated a little.

But instead of falling in with the mama cows and the Brahman heifers as it seemed they might do, the cow and the bull simply passed through the herd and emerged from the other side, like jaywalkers who pay no attention to the swirl of traffic that momentarily engulfs them. They continued up the rise on the opposite side of the draw from me. I gritted my teeth.

It is against the rules to "chouse" cattle unnecessarily. If your image of cowboys working cattle features a large cloud of dust hanging over what appears to be a barely controlled stampede, you have only the dust right. In this day and age, ranchers usually sell their beef by the pound, rather than by the head. They want their cattle to be fat and don't want them to die of heatstroke (to which fat cattle are naturally prone). Therefore, cattle are "eased" from one place to another whenever they will allow themselves to be eased. Nevertheless, the finer points of supply-side economics are sometimes wasted on the modern woman of twelve who is concerned about her image and whose blood is near the boiling point. The most satisfying revenge she can take on those responsible for her plight, if they happen to be cattle, is to chouse them—to fall in behind them at a dead run, a pace to which they are completely unaccustomed. Nothing gratifies quite like a "ruffled" cow.

And so, my sympathetic understanding of their distress having given way to anger in behalf of my own, I "lined" the cow and the bull out across the tops of the rises for a couple of hundred yards and then turned them down into the draw before slowing my horse to a trot. I figured they had learned their lesson and would surely join the rest of the bunch now; however, they simply blew into the cows at the bottom of the draw and kept on going, scattering the baby calves like seabirds and coming out the other side as they had done once before. My little bunch, which had on that first occasion maintained its identity *as* a bunch, now split neatly along its social seams, the three Brahman heifers roiling off down the draw like white steam. The five mama cows followed the same route but at a much slower rate, collecting and soothing their frightened babies and casting indignant looks in my direction.

The shattering of my bunch was the shattering of my hopes. Inevitably now, those knights in shining Stetsons (as they no doubt saw themselves) would come to save the damsel who had gotten herself into a mess (as they no doubt saw me). "I wish you'd mind your own dumb business," I muttered through clenched jaws, envisioning their cheery greetings and what was bound to be the upshot of this whole episode—the rendezvous at the trailers and the sniggering. "And drop dead," I added for good measure.

I was still charging recklessly about trying to regather the remainder of my herd when it occurred to me that the heifers' arrival *en déshabillé* at the windmill might actually speed up rather than delay the rescue. While it was true that stopping the heifers would use up time, as would the strategy session at the trough, it was also true that the distraught condition of the heifers would imply that my straits were very dire and would erase whatever uncertainties might have prevented the hands from setting out immediately to help me. They might even decide to let the heifers go. I imagined them peering intently at the runaways and concluding that my crisis was urgent enough to warrant immediate action.

As I did, my eyes became malicious slits through which I could see only the authors of my present woe, the cow and the bull. Having finally become winded, they had slowed to a trot and then stopped. I galloped back to hurry the mama cows along, devising ingenious tortures to inflict upon the aggravating pair as I went. When the mamas were sufficiently stirred up, I wheeled my horse around, nearly colliding with the three smiling young men who had ridden up behind me. "What's takin' ya so long?" one asked banteringly, having not yet gotten the picture, and I, too locked in my fury to care either about my image or two hundred years of mandatory custom, screamed in answer as I raced past him, "that f---ing cow and bull!"

And sure enough, as I rushed on toward the offensive creatures, I realized why they had stopped and that I had spoken truer than I knew.

4   *Roundup*

MANY TIMES DURING THE YEAR the rancher gathers part of his cattle for one reason or another—to move the Lake Pasture cattle to the East Trap during cocklebur season, for example, or to relocate the strays who refuse to stay off the neighbor's property. The two occasions when he gathers them all are called the Spring and Fall Roundups, appropriately so, as they occur in the general vicinity of those two seasons and as they are the cause of another annual ritual, the springing up of the rancher's leafy hopes in April when he sees the flock of new calves about to receive his brand, and the wilting of those same hopes in October when the prices the calves bring as "weaners" are substantially below what market analyses predicted they would be. Every year, year after year, the "unknown quantities"—the amount of weight the babies will gain in six months and the cents-per-pound cattle buyers will be willing to pay for that weight—invite much optimistic speculation; and every year, year after year, the numbers, as they become apparent, force the rancher to downgrade his image of himself as a "cattle baron" to "cattle knight" or perhaps just plain "cattle person, esquire." The inevitable concomitant of his diminished status is a deflated ego, and thus do the two major annual events on a ranch confirm the accuracy of the adage that cautions us not to be too surprised when what springs up falls right back down again.

But there are other aspects of rounding up than those that inspire grandiose visions of empire and rule and then cruelly dash them, aspects that account for the rancher's otherwise incomprehensible insistence on finding excuses to round up all the time. For one thing, rounding up is a significant literary event. It is a gathering not only of cows but of cowboys, cowgirls, and cowhorses during which anything can happen. The atmosphere, even though the conversation at the predawn breakfast table flows easily, is tense and expectant. Will a maverick steer break from the herd at some point and have to be roped? Will a fresh horse bog his head and try to buck off his rider? Will a fresh horse bog his head just as his rider has roped a maverick steer? Will the plunging steer run under the bucking horse or over the fallen rider? Everybody hopes so, and, indeed, the potential for some sort of entertaining disaster to occur (to someone else, of course) is great when a steer, a horse, and a cowboy are all in the same pasture, and it increases in direct proportion to the number of greenhorns and cowdogs who might show up. Out of these little incidents come roundup stories, without the accompaniment of which the more mundane tasks—fixing fence, windmilling, hauling hay—seem like real work. A supper without a story can't be redeemed even by fresh biscuits, and even the most creative yarn-spinner will get as predictable as the weather in Amarillo if he doesn't have, now and again, the inspiration of a new roundup.

Furthermore, if rounding up is a dismal lesson in the science of economics, it is an uplifting one in the study of philosophy. It forces the rancher to examine his *raison d'être* and goes some way toward clarifying, if not this specific ontological issue, at least some others much like it. Paradoxically, the very roundup that prompts the rancher in a financial mood to wonder why he stays in the cow business can instruct the reflective rancher in the virtues of rewards other than money. In the brisk morning air, the white clouds issuing from the cattle's nostrils remind the rancher that the goods in which he trades have life, and, having it, they touch his own in some positive way that diamonds, plumbing fixtures, or stocks and bonds cannot. The buying and selling of animals can, of course, blunt rather than nourish the soul, and there are surely ranchers to whom cattle become miniature factories—cogs and pulleys and tubes through which grass is run and converted (at least part of it) into dollars. Perhaps if that transformation were genuinely lucrative, more of these hardened Dickensian industrialist types would infest the profession. As it is, though frequently the adjective "wealthy" is affixed to the noun "rancher," the typical cattle operation repays investors in enriched moments rather than in enriched bank accounts—in the sorts of airy nothings that wiser heads are always telling young lovers they can't live on; in the kinds of profit not likely to attract those who habitually affix the adjectives "hard" and "cold" to the noun "cash."

Rounding up intensifies the contact with nature and

the outdoors that is the true rancher's true reward. The mother cow, in defiance of the horse and rider urging her down the trail, turns to protect the calf tagging wearily after her and to low encouragement to it. Two bulls paw dirt and bellow great oaths at one another, working themselves into a red rage that, at some ill-timed juncture, will erupt in a herd-scattering brawl. A half-grown heifer spies a tarantula crawling across the open ground, and forgetting in her curiosity everything else, drops her nose on the spider's back and trails it as it makes its stately progress directly beneath the neck of a startled cowhorse. A steer with an injured leg needing to be tended pauses to rest, his pain reflected in his dark eyes.

The inveterate realist can smile sardonically at these sentimental little roundup vignettes. No doubt most ranchers, who consider themselves more pragmatic than anyone, will never be candid about their feelings and will never confess that it is an abiding interest in the very life processes of their animals and of nature in general that keeps them from selling out and moving to the city. If you ask one why, if he's such a realist, he clings to a business that some say is obsolescent and that everybody knows is financially troubled, he'll invariably assume an "aw shucks" expression and tell you that he stays because he "donno how ta do anythang else." That is as much as to say that he doesn't *want* to do anything else and that the reasons are embarrassing and none of your affair.

Finally, rounding up is a good outlet for the rancher's physical and mental energies. It pits him against a worthy adversary, the cagey cow, as well as against circumstances particular to each individual roundup of terrain, amount and quality of available help, size and shape of pasture, and destination. To gather a pasture successfully, the rancher must be an inventive tactician, a skillful logician, and a cool-headed but inspiring leader of men and women. Although he is sometimes appalled to catch himself doing it, he must think like a cow, and simultaneously, like a cowhorse as well as a cowboy. Rounding up rekindles in him the primitive excitement of the hunt without exposing him to the dangers, all-too-prevalent during deer season, of some other over-eager hunter shooting his horse out from under him. It stirs the blood, relights the fire in his eye, recoils the spring in his step—is conducive, in short, to a livelier functioning of the vital bodily parts and thought processes. Although it may quell for yet another season his dreams of owning a ranch house like the one in "Giant" or "Dallas," it's good exercise. Besides, what's the use of having a bunch of cattle if you don't round them up once in awhile?

• • •

Behind every successful roundup is a good plan, although of course this might be said about the nether regions of many an unsuccessful one too. When I was a small child, the Heart-Diamond was to me a bewildering and limitless expanse of identical hills and mazy draws, and "the plan" was far too complicated for me to know it even existed, much less that I was a part of it. When I graduated from the pillow upon which I rode, usually asleep, in front of my mother, to my own old and gentle horse, one cowhand, usually my mother again, was assigned to watch over me and was, therefore, not much available to do anything else. My earliest contributions did not go far to offset the demands rounding up made on the energies and resources of the Heart-Diamond, and, indeed, it was the case that having me "help" was like having one good worker throw down her gloves and walk off.

From my preadolescent perspective, hunting cows was like hunting Easter eggs. You rode over here and picked up a red one to add to your collection and over there to get a motley-colored one, and when you had plenty, you took them all home. For a very long time, I thought my father called his cows "old hides" when he was angry with them because of their habit of lying very still behind a mesquite bush whenever a horse and rider approached.

When I got a little older, I began to realize that there *was* a plan and that everybody except me knew what it was, including the hired help, none of whom was familiar with the Heart-Diamond as I supposedly was by now. Some of the men who came to help us were not even "real" but only "weekend" cowboys, and occasionally one showed up wearing his spurs upside down or his Stetson hat creased peculiarly. But even these "dudes" seemed to see "the big picture" clearly, whereas I saw only random patches of color. I never wished to reveal my abysmal ignorance to these relative strangers by asking my father for more specific information, nor did my father wish me to reveal it either to them or to him. On roundup days, he was more distracted and less inclined than usual to entertain inquiries into the nature of the business at hand. He supposed that, since I had worked cattle in this pasture "a hundred times," I must surely know where we were headed and how we were going to get there. It was probably true that I *had* by now worked cattle in this pasture a hundred times, but his supposition had been founded (on a veritable earthquake of shaky ground) by my thirty-sixth or forty-ninth time and I *think* by as early as my first or second time. No amount of evidence to the contrary—and there was plenty—seemed to rock his faith that I "surely knew by now."

But I really didn't. The plan continued to be a puzzle for me, one for which I always lacked those few crucial pieces that, once in place, miraculously transform a hodgepodge of lines and brushstrokes into "The Garden at Versailles" or "Sunset over the Harbor." I had, nevertheless, to act on what I could make out. Once, for example, I deduced from various clues my close-mouthed father inadvertently let slip that we were "throwing" all the cattle toward the Middle Pasture. Never before had we rounded up High Lonesome in this manner. I knew from prior experience that prior experience meant nothing, but this one time I suppose it must have, for my cows and I ended up alone at the Middle Pasture gate. Another time, I thought I knew that we were to "pick up" only cows with unbranded baby calves and so, like a grown-up, I left behind everything else—"dry" cows, cows with branded calves, bulls—rather than indiscriminately driving in everything, as a child would do. I got to see the sights in my part of the pasture twice that day.

I decided in my early teens that men automatically intuited the plan the moment they came near it—that it sprang full-blown into their heads, attracted by the contours of their brains in which it saw for itself a perfect niche, and that women's niches and contours were not similarly inviting. Men, no matter how inexperienced as cowhands, never seemed to be at a loss to know what was expected of them, and naturally, their confident manner irritated the pearl of my insecurity and caused it to grow painfully large. Furthermore, although I really did know my way around the Heart-Diamond by now, the men's roundup assignments were always more prestigious than mine for reasons I could not fathom. I longed to be sent dashing off to the river, my horse's hooves clattering over the rocks as he flew along, but I usually got sent to the nearest corner or the shortest draw, or left to hold the cows who had already wandered in to the windmill on their own.

Still, I was growing wiser about the plan. I noticed, for example, that the men never actually asked outright questions about it, but would "sidle up" to it, approaching it softly and carefully as though it were a quivering colt ready to bolt at the least sudden sound or movement. "Reckin them ol' cows" (it is *de rigueur* for cowboys to be ungrammatical, so even the school teacher who occasionally helped us tried to sound as if he had failed the second grade and dropped out) "reckin them ol' cows we find on the river are gonna wanna go ta the windmill?" one of them might casually ask, as though he had no real interest in an answer and was only trying to pass the time.

"Donno," my father would reply after awhile, his mind attending to so many details that it had to rummage around up there for the words. "Maybe we better let 'em go on down the river 'til they hit the fence."

"Reckin that little gate's still a'settin' there at the top a' that hill."

(long pause) "Yep."

"Reckin they'll see the house from there."

"Might." (another long pause) "But that pen's a quarter mile south."

If each hand "reckined" enough—that is, if each probed subtly, delicately, but steadily—the outlines of the plan, like an ancient village under excavation, would slowly emerge, and if there were enough of these cowboy archaeologists, we'd all know what we were doing by the time we had ridden to the spot at which we were supposed to start doing it. Once I tried to chip in and, assuming what I thought to be the diffident mode of the men, allowed as to how I "reckined" we'd pick up the cows we'd just seen at the mouth of Dagger Draw on the way back. "I donno how we're gonna do that," my father said testily. "Surely you know by now that we aren't goin' anywhere near Dagger comin' back." When this final piece of the puzzle I had been constructing did not click into place, the rest of it fell apart, though nobody else seemed to care much that Dagger Draw had suddenly dropped out of the picture.

Then an incident occurred that finally did make a few things click into place. Education is always the rare and fortuitous convergence of a great delicacy and a palate neither too unsophisticated nor too jaded to appreciate it. Certainly fourteen is a knowing but unjaded age.

A man who earned his living as a forklift operator at the potash mines came out one weekend to help us round up. He was mounted on a small black horse he preposterously called Fury, who danced and bobbed excitedly through the first part of our trek to the back of the pasture and who, by the time we were actually ready to begin working, was already lathered and tired. Fury had probably never been ridden more than forty-five minutes at a stretch, and had, I supposed as I watched him being unloaded from the trailer, never seen a cow. Nevertheless, the man patted and talked to him as though he were a high-priced racehorse. Neither had the man ever seen a cow, I thought to myself contemptuously, and he wouldn't have known what to do with her if he had. He wore a new pair of chaps and sat rigidly upright in his saddle, his right hand making a point of never touching the saddle horn. Surely my father would make *him* stay at the windmill to hold the cattle and let me do something really important. I rode to the back of the pasture feeling less moody than usual.

Naturally, I was surprised and then outraged when my father, after handing out all the other assignments, sent the man on Fury to the west fenceline and me to the windmill. Tears started up in my eyes but not so many that I was denied the gratifying sight of this unspeakably green greenhorn heading off in the wrong direction. He would be sure to miss the lakey place near the northwestern corner of the pasture in which cattle loved to graze. What could you expect from somebody who named his horse "Fury"? I patted hard on the neck of my own horse, Pumpjack—so-called because his disproportionately long head made him resemble those large pumping mechanisms you see in Texas oil fields—and fought the lump in my throat. My father had already ridden away—"goin' ta the river," I imagined resentfully. I would not tell him until we got all the way to the house with the cattle that the greenhorn had not ridden far enough north to hit the low place. Then, casually, I would drop my little bomb. Somebody would have to ride all the way back to pick up the cattle that were almost invariably in that corner. I would not volunteer. With incessant loping and yelling, I kept the bewildered "windmill cows" in an unnecessarily tight knot for two hours or so.

The hands at last began to reappear, each driving a little bunch of cattle—except for the greenhorn who came high-loping up with nothing but a pleased grin on his face. I was certain my father would notice that he had no cows and that the hill he came off of should not have been on his route at all. When he stopped near me, I squelched a vicious urge to ask him "by the way" whether or not there had been much grass growing in the lakey place in the corner. His little horse was wringing wet, but the greenhorn did not seem fazed in the least that so much energy should have been so extravagantly and futilely spent.

As we started the cattle toward home, I heard him chattering like a magpie to my father about the magnificent performance of Fury—how the little horse had gamely plunged through the sandhills, which were tough on any horse, how with some work he'd make a great pasture horse, how his small size did not mean he couldn't do a big job. He declared that the pasture was beautiful back there ("you didn't see the best part," I muttered) and that he had ridden carefully by every clump of brush that might possibly conceal a cow. My father, I knew, was always put off by people who fished for compliments, and I fully expected him to find some pretext for riding to the other side of the herd, but he remained as long as the man talked, not saying much and nodding and smiling pleasantly in response to the narrative. The man was obviously excited by his morning's adventure and joked familiarly with the more experienced hands, while I, nursing my nascent grudge, rode in withdrawn silence.

A mile or so into the drive, my father, who by now had taken up his position as the outrider on my side of the herd, reined his horse to a halt, lowered his head, and removed his hat. I intended not to speak when I drew even with him, but he signaled me over with a minute gesture of his hand, which then settled quickly back on the horn of his saddle where it had been resting. "Along here somewhere," he said in a quiet voice, though nobody was near us, "why don'cha kinda drop back toward that big lakey place in the corner."

I looked at him blankly, but then, with the distinctive "plop" a small stone makes when you throw it into the water trough, a piece of some entirely different kind of puzzle—one that had perhaps been assembling itself all along in the recesses of my adolescent brain—dropped into a slot that had heretofore been vacant, and the first lines of an interesting new picture appeared. I do not know quite why I repressed the joyous outburst—"idiot-brain missed a buncha cattle, didn't he?"—that formed in my mind as the most immediate reaction to my father's instructions, but I did and said only "okay," though I loaded that brief utterance with as much significance as a brief utterance can carry. I turned my horse to go but then paused to hear what else my father was saying. "Why don'cha kinda angle around this way?" He gestured not quite in the direction of the west fenceline, his hand this time not losing contact with the saddle at all. "Ya can check that little draw right over the hill, too, if ya go that way."

"Okay," I said again, this time with no inflection whatsoever, as though I were entirely accustomed to such orders. But I had had one of those stunning flashes of insight usually reserved for, if not always appreciated by, the characters in a Greek tragedy, and I saw by its light that my father had confidence in my ability to do a job as well as a man—that, in fact, he thought I could handle something a man hadn't been able to handle. Instead of being the "outsider"—the lowest profile on the cowboy version of the totem pole—as I had always felt myself to be on roundup days, I was in league with my father against another who, I realized, had been the outsider all along. I was amazed. I saw myself catching up with the main herd, driving at a hasty trot the cows the man on Fury had not found. Somehow, I'd make him know that the mistake had been his and that I had been chosen to repair the damage.

"If ya find any cattle,"—my father's voice interrupted this pleasant reverie—"why don'cha jus' put 'em through that gate into the trap. We'll get 'em later." The stunning flash had apparently left a few corners unilluminated. It would make more sense to bring any cows I found up to the herd, and thus we would have them where we needed them to be. However, the contemplative set of his face, as well as memories of previous, less-than-welcome critiques of his methods, prevented me from pointing out to my father the inconsistency in his logic, even though I was disappointed that I would not get to rub the greenhorn's nose in his egregious error.

But then I had another flash, this one more bright and stunning than the first. My father was, for some reason, protecting the greenhorn from something and did not think, as I did, that he needed to be taught a lesson. I was not certain I understood all the complexities of my father's motives and imagined that, were I in his place, I'd have thrown a rope under the greenhorn's horse to see if he'd buck. But maybe there was more to the man on the little black horse than met the eye. I'd think about him on the way to the fenceline. What I *did* understand was that I was being let in on a secret, a very adult secret, and that it was being assumed I was adult enough to appreciate how sensitive a secret it was.

Most important to me at the moment, however, was that I was being entrusted with a meaningful job. Welling up in place of all my resentment was a warm gratitude to my father and tremendous pride that, at last, I had earned my way into the closed circle of those "in the know" and was at this moment being initiated into the mysteries of the cult. Wishing to exercise the long-awaited privileges of membership immediately, I casually but confidently "reckined" I'd just leave the yearlings and bring everything else. "Now why on earth would ya wanna do that?" my father snapped before riding off in a cloud of dust.

• • •

I know now that, in theory at least, rounding up is as simple as sweeping the floor, a chore to which it might, in fact, be instructively compared. Your approach to sweeping the living room floor (for example) will be dictated by a number of variables, including the shape of the room, the location of the furniture in it, and your final destination. Let's say you wish to "pen" your pile of dust and dirt near the coffee table in the center of the room. You'll probably sweep toward your destination from each of the four corners, a job you'll complete much faster if you have three friends with brooms to help you. You don't ever want to buck nature if you don't have to, however, so if a stiff breeze is blowing through the window, you'll probably choose a collecting point somewhere in the south end, in which case you'll begin at the northern baseboards, crossing and recrossing the width of the room to keep the swelling line of filth advancing evenly.

Similarly, it is easier to drive cattle down a smooth though meandering trail than to take the rocky shortcut; it is easier to drive them toward their watering spots than away from them (for which reason ranchers frequently build their holding pens at windmills and water holes);

and it is easier to find them early in the morning when they're out grazing than in the heat of the day when they're "shaded up." Cattle don't like traveling into the wind any more than dust does, but sometimes you have to make them, which is why sweeping the floor is generally a little easier than working cattle. Again, the efficacy of any strategy is greatly enhanced by additional brooms. It therefore behooves you to get along with those of your neighbors who might happen to own one and to help them whenever they need to sweep.

Regardless of the basic blueprint on which you model your approach, you know that the keys to a clean living room floor are a tranquil mind and a flexible personality. You don't go to pieces if you have to swerve off course to get your dirt around a reclining chair; if the room, rather than being perfectly symmetrical, is perfectly asymmetrical; if the bristles on one side of your broom don't seem quite as "conscientious" about getting all the dirt as the bristles on the other side; or if you discover, two-thirds of the way down the floor, that you've overlooked a tiny pocket of dust bunnies hiding behind the sofa where you started. You make adjustments.

Probably the most foolproof roundup plan is the "Big Game Hunt." To implement it, the rancher must have enough cowboys that he can line them up side by side across the entire width of the pasture. In this formation, they ride slowly forward, driving all the cattle before them into large nets. The Big Game Hunt (in keeping with the spirit of our original metaphor, we might call it the "Industrial Broom Sweep") is a highly effective technique that generally "nets" all the cows in the pasture, although a few may manage to slip behind the lines when a cowboy looks down to light a cigarette. Most ranchers, however, do not use this plan, claiming it is simply too efficient and takes all the fun out of working cattle. But it is more likely the case that few ranchers are on speaking terms with enough neighbors to muster the numbers requisite for spanning the width of their milk-cow pen, much less their largest pastures.

The "Fan Plan" is available to the moderately agreeable rancher. The idea here is for all hands to ride together to the starting point and then "fan out." A real cowboy, priding himself in his plainspokenness, would never use a phrase so poetical—"I'll go thisaway, ya'll go thataway," he'd say without a trace of a metaphor—but the image of a fan folding and unfolding represents fairly accurately this method of gathering cattle. Arriving at the back of the pasture in a little cluster of hats and horses, the cowboys separate suddenly, spacing themselves at intervals along the fence. The Fan Plan resembles a Big Game Hunt with lots of holes in it, obviously, but instead of merely riding forward in a straight line and thus not finding any of the cows grazing in the gap between himself and the next rider, each hand follows a more or less serpentine route through his "corridor," carefully combing those brushy spots and little draws in which a cow might be hiding.

The person on the trail to the pens is the "backbone" of the fan, for it is to him that cattle are gradually "thrown" as the drive progresses. As he pushes along what cows he already has, he watches for the riders on either side of him to "shove" the cows they have found toward him. If he sees cattle coming his way, he lopes over to get them, first giving his own bunch a little scare to keep it moving while he's gone. When the second cowboy is certain he sees the first one coming to relieve him of his cattle, he "drops over" (after giving *his* cows a good scare) until he spots the cowboy next to *him*. If the third cowboy has started cattle toward the second, the second lopes to get them and shoves them toward the first. This pattern is more or less duplicated across the width of the pasture, and thus the fan opens and closes with an undulating motion as each cowboy makes gradual forward progress while simultaneously zigzagging through his corridor and "feeding" all the cows into the main herd.

There are a couple of drawbacks to this technique. One is that it requires each cowboy to estimate pretty accurately the location of all his colleagues and the speed at which they and their cattle are probably moving through the pasture. Good hands have no real difficulty seeing the entire operation in their mind's eye or compensating for any minor flaws and hitches either in their own performance or in the performance of another hand. Bad ones get to the windmill an hour early or an hour late, having left behind the cattle they were supposed to pick up and ridden through country somebody else had already searched.

The second problem with The Fan Plan is that cows do not always comprehend clearly what they are supposed to do—or comprehend all too well. They may be in high gear when cowboy #2, after whistling at them a last encouraging time, leaves them for cowboy #1 to pick up, but they will not necessarily maintain this heady pace and may even stop dead, like sailboats abruptly becalmed. Cowboy #1 must, therefore, traverse the entire distance between his bunch of cattle and them, which in most instances is quite considerable. Or they may pick up speed as, rapidly completing a 180 degree turn, they flee back to those very bushes out of which they have just been so painstakingly plucked. Or they may decide to do a little fanning out themselves. The "Partially Collapsed Fan" occurs when all the cows on one side of the pasture follow the rules, while all those on the other side do not.

In the "Modified Fan Plan" (sometimes called "The Sieve"), each hand throws his cattle toward the corridor where the next rider would be if there *were* a next rider. Before abandoning them to "drop over," he hollers loudly, slaps his chaps with his hand in a threatening manner, and warns them that a rabble of supermarket shoppers in search of bargain hamburger has been spotted in the vicinity. If this ploy works, the cattle gallop right through the empty corridor and into an occupied one, but it hardly ever does.

At the Heart-Diamond, we were customarily so shorthanded that the Modified Fan Plan had to be modified even more; it was usually altered so radically, in fact, that, had one of our roundups been viewed by a spectator seated on a cloud, it might have resembled the maddened scramble of small children hunting for Easter eggs. However, as has been suggested already, the essential ingredient of a good plan is adaptability. Rigid adherence to any initial scheme is sure death. So what might have appeared to be chaos and confusion was actually the fluid motions of the plan as it bent, buckled, and reconstituted itself to circumvent a cliff (which cannot, after all, be relocated as easily and conveniently as a reclining chair) or to regather cows that, if they had not been scattered like dust *by* the four winds, had most likely been scattered (by something) *to* them.

• • •

Before you drive cattle anywhere, you have to find them. If you live in those parts of the world where the land is level, the grass ample, and the pastures small, all you have to do is buy a tall horse. On roundup days, you ride to the back side, stand up in your stirrups, and note the location of each cow. But on the Heart-Diamond, the fact that you might be able to see five miles to the next large draw does not mean you don't have to ride those five miles and search that draw, because each cow has about sixty-four acres of hills, draws, low places, and brush in which to lose herself, and because cows cleverly disguise themselves as bushes or boulders. Furthermore, the Heart-Diamond features large, white boulders, presumably thrown up by some ancient upheaval of the earth. In fact, I had never noticed how many large white boulders lay strewn about our pastures until my father bought some Charolais cows, then in fashion among ranchers and cow buyers the way French designer jeans were, for a time, among teenagers. Their many virtues included a brilliant white color, which, we all thought excitedly, would be much easier to see than the blacks, browns, and reds sported by the other breeds we raised, all of which tended to match too closely the colors of our vegetation and soil.

I, in particular, was overjoyed by the purchase of the Charolais herd, for I had always had more trouble than anyone distinguishing a black cow from a dark green bush at any distance of more than seventy-five yards and always had to ride right up to the object in question to see whether or not it was breathing. My father instructed me repeatedly to focus carefully on anything I thought might be a cow, for if it were, it would, in a relatively short time, flick an ear. My father, however, had 20-20 vision, and when he stared out over the pasture, its contents did not swim before him in sinuous waves. Stopping his horse, he would peer at and soon identify some dark blotch a mile away, his startlingly light blue eyes then sweeping easily over the rest of the landscape, ferreting out and identifying any other dark blotches lurking therein. Outlined against the turquoise western sky, he cut—at least I thought he did—a dashing, movie-cowboy figure, though probably his features were not quite rugged enough or sufficiently "serious" to win him a role. Too much good humor lurked at the corners of his mouth, and when he spoke, his facial expressions were too mobile and actually betrayed his real feelings. Nevertheless, his skin (the few parts of it not covered by the invariably long-sleeved, western shirt, chaps, and Stetson hat) was a golden bronze, his manner easy and confident.

I, by contrast, in addition to being a girl and therefore automatically excluded from the "dashing figure" set, was round-faced, nearsighted to the point of blindness, and buck-toothed to boot. Spying a dark blotch on the horizon, I would squint prodigiously, wrinkling my nose to keep in place my thick-lensed cat-eye glasses (cat-eye glasses, vaguely French, were in vogue then too, along with Charolais). So much concentration of attention and energy on the muscles in the upper hemisphere of my face left none to spare on the muscles in the lower hemisphere, which, therefore, did nothing. Consequently, my jaws would slacken and my mouth drop open, exposing my buck teeth. I did not resemble a movie cowboy, or even Dale Evans, and my sister, constantly catching me in this pose, never let it go unremarked. "Gaa, ya look dorkey," she'd say ("Gaa" and "dorkey" were both "in" expressions that year), her own finely chiseled features incapable of arranging themselves so as to make her look ridiculous even if she had wanted them to.

I was certain the Charolais would improve my life.

But even my father admitted after a couple of cow works that the Charolais posed a problem. Specifically, the sun glinted off their white bodies, making them virtually indistinguishable from the white boulders, off of which the sun also glinted. Perhaps even worse, the cows were possessed of an uncanny ability to stand absolutely still for hours on end. Nature seemed, in their case, to have suspended that law regulating the involuntary muscle spasms of the bovine ear upon which we had heretofore relied so heavily. Their statuelike immobility baffled our minds as well as our eyes, for we could not conceive what narrow byway in the broad course of cow evolution had led the Charolais to possess such a peculiarly uncowlike (and unhandy) trait. We finally decided it was probably something French and therefore not surprisingly nonsensical.

At any rate, these two features—a complete absence of involuntary movements of any kind and a brilliant whiteness—wreaked much havoc with our roundups and cost us many a profitless cross-country trek. Eventually, we began to breed our French cattle to plain old Hereford bulls, who, though originally English and possessed of a few quirks of their own, at least had the good sense to move their ears occasionally. We also anticipated that a cross between a white Charolais and a red Hereford would produce a showy, highly visible pink; but no doubt because of some defect in the genes of the Charolais, the calves came out a dirty yellow, about the color of sand dunes, which are ubiquitous in the Southwest.

Thus were dashed my hopes for an improved life. In fact, I had to wear braces for three years before my sister stopped calling me a dork.

• • •

Although the repertoire of every cowboy features some stories of the ones that got away, eight times out of ten a human being, even one of middling capabilities, mounted on a fast, intelligent cowhorse, can successfully get to where he wants to get to with the cows he wants to get there with. The occasional renegade becomes more tractable after she discovers herself to be at the end of a rope, the opposite end of which is attached to a horse who nonchalantly watches her while she bellows and bounces around. Still, it is remarkable that so few cows are mavericks and that a single rider can usually control the movements of ten, twenty, fifty, or even a hundred of them. One angry heifer can run only one direction, but fifty heifers could, with a little preplanning, scatter in fifty different directions, cramping the style of even the swiftest, most willing horse. That such rebellions do not break out often and that cows do not, in other respects, exploit their superior numbers, has partly to do with the "herding instinct," which prompts every cow to spook and run over the edge of the cliff if one does. In other words, if the cowboy can convince the leader cow that moving from the East Trap to the Lake Pasture will be greatly to her advantage, the rest of the herd will generally acquiesce in the plan. The herding instinct is nature's way of evening the odds against the cowboy.

On the other hand, though humans might in some sense have won the roundup game when they slam the gate closed on the last straggling mama cow indulging her impertinently playful baby, in another sense, they never win, for each roundup chips a little more off the coating of patient endurance of trials and tribulations that protects us all from madness. The modern cow does not stampede as frequently as her less gentle, long-horned predecessor of the trail-driving era, resorting instead to the subtler tactics of psychological warfare. The cows that get away from today's cowboy don't go in for a lot of hoopla. They simply aggravate him to the brink of self-destruction, like a leaky faucet or the first rattle in a new car.

Still, cows do generally allow themselves at last to be rounded up, penned, branded, doctored, and ultimately shipped to the packing house. They understand that, were it not for their vital role in the human food chain, they'd probably be extinct (or virtually so). Although cows can become docile and loving creatures and certainly do not mind being fed two or three times a day, they make cumbersome pets. There's always a bunch of bulls in the china closet if you forget and leave the door open. Neither are cows big draws at zoos or circuses, having no particularly noteworthy talent other than cud-chewing, which wears thin after awhile. If they give purpose and meaning to the life of the rancher, he returns the favor, conferring on them not so much status as would get them hunted into oblivion, à la the passenger pigeon, whose feathers were thought to be much too good for the likes of a silly bird, nor so little that they are regarded as vermin and therefore dispensable. Cows "mean" to just the right degree, and out of gratitude to the rancher who has defined their role on the planet so concisely, they permit him the illusion that he is in charge of his ranch.

5   *The Voice*

MY FATHER ONCE READ AN ADVERTISEMENT in an eastern catalog for a device called a gravity pump. This miracle of high technology could convert even the most gentle downhill gradation of a stream into a remarkably steep and high upward flow, using only the energy generated by the falling water itself. Its relatively few moving parts were supposed never to rust or wear out.

As luck would have it, the perfect spot to plug in a gravity pump was in the back of one of our pastures. A little creek to which the cattle in this particular pasture had to go for water tumbled down a narrow canyon whose sheer sides made access to the creek difficult. Not relishing the strenuous walk up and down the rocky trail, most of the herd tended to stay in the canyon near their favorite watering hole on the creek, subsisting on the relatively sparse growth nearby rather than fattening themselves on the good grazing "out top." For this reason, and because he liked unique and ingenious gadgets, my father suspended his general skepticism about things "Yankee" in origin, ordered a gravity pump, and, when it arrived, set about installing it to send water from the watering hole in the canyon—a widening in the creek beneath some cottonwood trees—straight up to the rim above.

Assembling the pump did not prove to be particularly difficult, but conveying the parts and lengths of PVC pipe down to the water hole before assembly did. Although they could be hauled to the canyon rim in the back of the pickup truck, more primitive means of locomotion had to be resorted to beyond that point, and so my parents each made one trip down the precipitous trail on foot, toting some of the lighter components of the pump and wondering what they were going to do about the heavier ones. My mother set her load down on the edge of the creek, and, wiping the sweat off her brow with a gloved hand, conveyed to my father with an articulate glance what she'd just as soon *not* do again. My father was also reluctant to repeat the trip on foot, so they rode horseback the next day to the spot at the rim of the canyon where they had left the remaining pieces of the pump in a neat stack. My mother dismounted, tied her horse to the limbs of a small bush, and began to hand up to my father, who was sitting astride his favorite horse, Beezlebomb, a red box containing some crucial fittings. The idea was that he'd carry it down the trail in front of him, balanced on the saddle horn, and then come back for another load. As there was nobody left to hand a box up to my mother, she would simply wait for my father to return, whereupon she'd load him up again.

Beezlebomb, a prudent horse, was suspicious of anything novel or irregular, and he apparently put the box into one of these classifications. He snorted, rolled his eyes, and ran several steps backward to express his displeasure each time my mother approached him. My father managed to grasp the proffered object without being unseated, but Beezlebomb subsequently refused to watch the trail very carefully, feeling obliged to keep one fearful eye turned back on the box at all times, with the result that there was much stumbling on his part and much concern on my father's that he and horse and fittings might topple off the face of the cliff. Six or seven voyages, each of them as perilous as the first, were necessary to get all the parts down into the canyon, though once they arrived there and were bolted and glued together, the pump functioned perfectly. The specially designed plastic pipe that spanned the distance between the creek and the new aluminum water trough up above formed the third leg of a right triangle whose other two limbs were the floor and the wall of the canyon.

My father had thought, before he received from the Pennsylvania Manufacturing Company the brochure describing its pump, that he'd probably have to get around to drilling a well and erecting a windmill somewhere in the sections of pasture above the canyon. He had hesitated to take this step partly because drilling a well is always a risky and costly venture, but mainly because the Heart-Diamond already featured four windmills. A fifth, though it might well enhance the quality of his cows' lives, was very likely to compromise the quality of his own. Compared with most other mechanisms, windmills are wonderfully uncomplicated and highly efficient—on the order of the hand-operated can opener, for example, or a pair of good wire pliers. Nevertheless, they are forever breaking down and needing repairs. The red-rod snaps in two during high winds, the leathers rot, the bottom cylinder rusts. Hunters, waiting to ambush the dove and quail who must come to the wells for water, drop pebbles into the well casing to pass the time, or shoot holes in the fan when the birds fail to show, or chop down the tower for firewood. For all its simplicity, a windmill is vulnerable to the ravages of time, weather, and thoughtless human beings.

Still, my father liked windmills and would have been in favor of buying a new one if he had thought he might be able to fix it by himself whenever it broke down, but he knew he couldn't do that. He knew too that my mother would be the person he'd have to ask for help. Ordinarily, he liked and appreciated my mother's help. She was more capable than virtually anyone else he knew, and her relaxed manner balanced well with his own (at times such as these) more "intense" personality. A "city girl"—she had grown up in the West Texas town of Marfa; population, about 2,500—she had adapted completely to the different demands of country living, and she enjoyed working with my father . . . usually.

Something happened to my mother when she "windmilled" with my father, something my father understood nothing about except that it always resulted in a quarrel. In truth, for my parents to try to fix a broken windmill without fighting was invariably a quixotic quest, a tilting at windmills, so to speak. Thirty years of marriage at about four windmillings per year had destroyed any illusions they might once have entertained that a bottom check would some day be releathered or a suckerod replaced in an atmosphere of mutual equanimity. Simply put, windmilling meant bad feelings—no ifs, ands, or buts—and my parents dreaded the days that a good breeze failed to fill one of the tanks scattered around the Heart-Diamond.

Actually, it is not surprising that windmilling puts a strain on relationships, even good ones. Only the Southwesterner's hyperconscientious observance of social proprieties prevents full-scale war from erupting between two windmilling neighbors who, in other cooperative ventures—branding, rounding up, building fence—have no trouble being civil to one another for hours at a time. Windmilling, however, is a tedious and somewhat dangerous job. It would get done more efficiently and with less friction if a complete and precise communication among its participants were possible. But telling anybody anything, anathema to most ranchers under the best of circumstances, is extremely difficult under these. One person (at least) must stand beneath the windmill tower amidst the whirring and banging of pulleys and pipes, while another sits thirty yards away in a pickup whose motor runs continuously. Messages, then, are conveyed via much hollering and many excited hand signals. The driver of the pickup, which is attached to a block-and-tackle (which, in turn, is attached to the pipes or suck-erods being hauled up out of or put back into the well), must drive forward or backward or slam on the brakes, all in immediate response to commands issued by the person under the tower, who, with very large and heavy wrenches, is attempting to uncouple (or rejoin if the well is being put back together) the sections of pipe or rod. If the driver mistakes a "whoa" for a "go," or if the wielder of the wrenches is in the wrong place when the pickup suddenly lurches forward, fingers can get amputated and ribs caved in. During one notorious windmilling on the ranch next to the Heart-Diamond, the tower person's foot became entangled in the tackle, and he was jerked to the top of the tower where he dangled upside down for awhile, along with a suckerod that was supposed to be up there.

Add to the constant pressure of having to be careful, then, the habit of pickups to stall when the clutch isn't released just so, the difficulty for the driver of interpreting the gestures and signals he must read in the rearview mirror while simultaneously dodging the mesquite bushes and cacti growing in the pickup's requisite path, the seemingly endless string of pipes or suckerods (or both) that must be raised up out of the well and then lowered back into it, and the natural tendency for verbal exchanges commenced in loud voices to escalate to even louder ones, and you have a potent formula for not having a very good time.

It is surely to my mother's credit, then, that none of the irritants that generally undermined the aplomb and good humor with which most windmillers at least begin the day ever bothered her much, not even the sweltering heat seeping through the floorboards of the pickup. What "got" to her was my father's voice raised in a shout, and it was not so much that he was shouting as that the timbre of the voice itself (not its tone or its meaning) rubbed her the wrong way. For that same inexplicable reason that some people cannot abide the squeal of fingernails scraped across a blackboard, my mother could not prevent the muscles in the back of her neck from tensing up (or the tiny hairs growing back there from rising) whenever my father hollered at her to "whoa" or "go." Tense neck muscles inevitably led to a headache and a headache to the general decay of my mother's nerves, not to mention her mood.

My father's voice was ordinarily soft, low, and gentle. It was not designed for use in shouting or even for pitching above the barely audible. When it *was* raised, the system that produced it, at least according to my mother's sensitive ears, suffered much stress and began to crack and strain and to emit erratic little shrieks and whistles at the ends of certain words. When it shouted, my father's voice stretched like chewed gum pulled between the fingers, grew thin and transparent, and eventually snapped in two. My mother categorized it with such sounds as the high notes on a poorly played violin, the squall of a Siamese cat, and the piercing "skree" of an ungreased windmill wheel, though other people did not act as if it were that bad.

She wished she could explain to my father why windmilling affected her the way it did, but she could not imagine where she'd go with the conversation once she'd said "the sound of your voice makes the filling in my tooth ache." He was a man who liked solid reasons, and this one, she admitted to herself, was pretty flimsy. Besides, his feelings would probably be hurt. And so she tried simply to "bear up," but even the very first "go!" would evoke the sensations in the back of her neck. By the third or fourth, she'd find herself losing her composure and uncontrollably answering the shouted instructions:

My father: Go!

My mother: I'm going, for Pete's sake!

At first my father would be perplexed by the Jekyll/Hyde transformation of her personality, but as temperatures grew warmer, her foul humor merely hastened the spoiling of his own, until eventually, he'd begin answering her answers:

My father: Whoa!

My mother: I'm whoaing, durn it! (My mother was too polite to actually swear, but replacing the "a" in "darn" with a "u" converts that mild expletive into real profanity, or at least my father, in his windmilling "mode," had difficulty detecting any difference between "durn it" and "damn you.")

My father: Well, thanks a lot! You like t'uv cut my hand off!!

My mother: What?

My father: I said, stop grindin' the gears in that outfit and watch what yer doin'!

My mother: You don't have to shout!

My father would treat this inevitable protest as a patent absurdity, for, of course, he *did* have to shout . . . especially now if he wanted the full ironical effect of his "explanation" to my mother that shouting was necessary ("you want me ta write letters instead?") to sink in. Halfway through this dialogue, my mother would be on the verge of flipping off the ignition, jumping out of the pickup, and stalking to the house. But the house was rarely in convenient stalking distance, and, as it is difficult to sustain the drama of an angry exit for four or five miles, she usually had to content herself with a good stomp on the brake or the gas pedal, which her rapidly boiling imagination may have transformed into some vulnerable section of my father's anatomy.

But if the windmilling lasted awhile, my father's voice, a comparatively weak instrument, would grow raspy and gradually disappear altogether, forcing him to rely solely on hand signals, which were expressive enough to impart quite eloquently his total disgust and chagrin but were somewhat more confining than his vocabulary. And, amazingly, even though he might be waving his arms furiously at her (at the very height of his wrath he'd take off his Stetson and signal with it, exaggerating the "stop" and "go" motions as though he were teaching them to a three-year-old), my mother would, as soon as my father's voice croaked its last order, recover her good humor. The final few suckerods would come gliding out of the well as sweetly as my father could have wished had he been in any condition by this time to appreciate such amenities. It was not really a conscious strategy on my mother's part to aggravate my father into "ruining" his voice, but sometimes she'd catch herself yelling "huh?" out the window of the pickup in response to an order that she had in fact heard quite plainly. It's little wonder then that my father (who regained his voice in a day but generally had no disposition to use it again for three or four) considered the gravity pump a lucky find, a miracle cure developed by wizards living in the mystical land of Pennsylvania.

Some time after he had installed the system, however, he discovered the rim trough to be empty and the cattle he'd driven up out of the canyon to be milling around their old water hole in the shade of the cottonwood trees. He rode down the trail and found the intake valve and pipe of the gravity pump pushed deep into the mud. Some "die hard" fans of the canyon—the herd would of course contain a few of these—had probably returned to their old stomping grounds the moment my father had ridden out of sight and had proceeded to stomp, inadvertently (to give them the benefit of the doubt) sinking the pipe. My father knew perfectly well that the habits of these rabid traditionalist types were not likely to change. He was around fifty or so himself and was beginning to become set in his ways, although the purchase of the gravity pump proved that he was still open to new developments and novel ideas. But these few old cows weren't, and rather than counting on them to stay out on top where he put them, he took steps to protect the pump, digging the mouth of the pipe out of the creek bed and placing beneath it a huge flat rock, which he pushed deeply enough into the mud to maintain a sufficient angle between the fall of the water and the pumping mechanism.

But several days later the trough was empty again, and the flat rock, along with the pipe, had settled out of sight in the black ooze. This time he placed beneath the pipe a double layer of rock and tamped it down into the creek bed, the theory being that somewhere down there was solid ground—a groundless theory, as it turned out, or at least one whose foundations would have to rest on something more substantial than two layers of rock, for the next time he checked it, the pipe was again submerged in mud. Some large creature, a bull perhaps, had probably stood on the rocks while drinking, oblivious to the settling of his front end as he took on ballast. My father once more dug out and propped up the pipe, but figuring he couldn't sink flat rocks all the way to China, he also piled several large tree limbs and some brush around the pump in such a way that they vaguely resembled a fence. Cows are not particularly intimidated by most fences, but many cows seem to respect the concept of one and will hesitate to violate a barrier symbolic of that concept. So far, my father was still pleased with his eastern purchase. Although it had cost him more time and effort than he had foreseen, it would eventually pay off, preventing much wear and tear on his marriage.

The creature, whatever he or she was, apparently had no special reverence for symbolism and a week later had strolled through the "fence," clearing a path that the other cattle supposed they might as well use as long as it was there. Only the real thing, my father realized, would impress the callous wrecker of his water project, and so he dropped over the edge of the canyon a roll of barbed wire and a number of posts, out of which he erected a very material and stern fence, one whose barbs were sharp enough to get the attention of even the most outlawed, fringes-of-society, criminal bull. Sure enough, the rim trough remained full long enough for the cattle who were ever going to do so to make the physical and psychological transition from the bottom of the canyon to the country on top, so that when it dried up again, they lingered in its vicinity, perfectly confident that the stream of water wont to flow into the trough would reappear before they died of thirst.

In his effort to justify their naive faith, my father went down to see what had gone awry this time and found in the ten-foot-square enclosure not only the pump but also a huge, brown-red Hereford bull, who, with front hooves planted firmly on the flat rocks, casually chewed his cud. So bulky was he that he seemed to wear the pen like armor, and, indeed, his size would have enabled him to indulge a warlike temperament if he'd been inclined to do so. But, not uncharacteristically for a bull, he was a placid, peaceable brute. He had not torn down the new fence, only scratched through it, as the tufts of hair hanging from the barbs and the sagging middle wire testified. Probably, he'd had a terrible itch on the back of his neck that he figured he'd cure by inserting his head between two wires and scratching against the top one. The fence's high-powered barbs no doubt felt so good that he had thrust his body a little further through to get at the grubs on his back. Then (much to his surprise, of course), the middle wire had stretched and finally popped off the posts, and he had (more or less) "fallen" through the fence, which would doubtlessly have turned him back if he had been charging rather than scratching. Thus do the meek inherit the earth. The bull offered no explanations or apologies, and, in fact, far from blushing at having been caught "red-handed," he gazed benignly at my father as if to thank him for remodeling the water hole—for tiling the baths and installing a backscratcher so conveniently adjacent thereto. To his mind, the spot under the shady trees was beginning to resemble a comfortable gentleman's club—just exactly what the neighborhood needed.

Although the idea occurred to him, my father could not shoot the bull, for his pedigree was impeccable and had cost a pretty penny. With forced calm, my father removed the several staples still holding up the middle wire and thus created a hole large enough to accommodate Fizzy's exit (the bull's name was Fizzy) even more comfortably than the hole that he had created for himself had accommodated his entrance. After my father screamed at him and chunked a couple of rocks in his direction, Fizzy finally took his leisurely leave, allowing the top wire to brush one last delicious time the length of his broad back before he ambled off down the canyon to await future developments.

My father sat down on a dried mesquite root, removed his hat, and passed his fingers through his brown hair, all signs that he was thinking. The brain needs air and a gentle tickle to get started again after being cooped up in a Stetson. The gravity pump was turning into a nuisance. Clearly, more radical measures than any he'd taken so far were needed to protect it. He still balked, however, at the idea of replacing it with a windmill, especially now that he'd already invested so much time and money in it. He swatted a fly, his blue eyes staring blankly at the toe of his boot, which, more or less of its own volition, was busy inscribing a semicircular arch in the dirt. He began to pay attention to what his foot was up to and in a little while exclaimed suddenly "a dome, of course!"

He decided to build a rock and mortar dome over the entire pump. The project would require some fairly sophisticated engineering skills but was certainly not beyond his ken, for he and my mother had designed and constructed all the rock and mortar water tanks on the Heart-Diamond. Furthermore, most of the materials needed for such a structure were to be had in the immediate vicinity of the pump. Hundreds of large, flat rocks, similar to the ones he had already sunk into the creek bed, littered the floor of the canyon, and the water and sand needed for mixing with cement to make mortar could be obtained right from the creek. Only the cement itself and the necessary tools would somehow have to be gotten to the site. My father recalled Beezlebomb and the red box and shook his head. A better method would have to be devised for transporting the fifty-pound bags of cement, especially since the construction of the pump house (in my father's mind's eye, the dome had blossomed into a neat little pump house) might require several of them. But obstacles were always to be expected whenever anything worth doing got done, and he'd think of something.

Liking his plan in spite of its one weak spot, my father replaced his hat and went home to submit the idea to my mother. She liked it too and thought a pump house would be prettier than a barbed wire fence, and, although my father supposed it was just like a woman to appreciate the aesthetic rather than the utilitarian genius of an idea, he was pleased that she was pleased. The cement was purchased during the next trip to town and stored in the barn, where it sat for two or three months, other chores having assumed priority over the construction project, especially since the fence seemed to be working now. The few cows who remained in the canyon found a new water hole near the old one, and Fizzy lit out for the country "on top," which now offered a wider selection from which to choose a harem.

Why my father decided to go ahead with the pump house is something of a mystery. Maybe he, too, secretly disliked the pen and thought it an eyesore—a jagged scar across the pristine cheek of the canyon; or maybe he did not want to waste the cement. Most likely, the image of the little pump house had seized his imagination and would not let go until it had seen itself realized in the physical world. The idea, in other words, and not the cement, is what my father did not want to waste.

At any rate, one day in early December, after the fall roundups were over, my father proposed to my mother that they load the tools and cement into the back of the pickup, haul them to the rim of the canyon, and then use the pickup to get them down to the water hole. My mother was perplexed by the last part of this plan—the vague part—but she knew that a bunch of questions, in the answering of which my father would have to draw on what he deemed a limited and precious supply of words, would make him grumpy. The day was gorgeous, as December days frequently are in southern New Mexico, and she was tired of being indoors, so she agreed to go along. Almost immediately, however, she regretted her decision. She felt strangely ill at ease not knowing what my father had in mind. Perhaps he intended to drive the pickup down into the canyon somehow. "Oh, he wouldn't do that," she scolded herself, uncertain, on the other hand, just what he would do. And "something," that anonymous messenger whose business it is to forewarn us of catastrophes, told her she wasn't going to like whatever it was.

After a long and bumpy ride, my parents arrived at the rim of the canyon directly above the water hole. They got out of the pickup, and, as he began to knot together four manila ropes, my father described to my mother his now fully formulated strategy for "transporting" the bags of cement to the water hole. He would tie one end of the 120-foot line he was in the process of creating out of the old ropes around a sack and the other end around the front bumper of the pickup. Then, my mother would drive slowly toward the rim, thus lowering the cement over the edge and down to where he would be waiting to catch and untie it. My mother experienced a tingling sensation in the back of her neck and was immediately opposed to the idea, but she still couldn't trace her anxiety to any specific source. She supposed she was just nervous about driving toward the steep drop-off. What if the brakes failed? What if she couldn't tell when to stop? She protested feebly as my father dangled the first bag over the rim. "Don' worry," he assured her, "I'll yell 'whoa' when ya've come far enough."

A complete understanding of any situation usually comes only after we're in it—too late for us to do much more than wish we were somewhere else. Now that my mother realized what her instincts had been whispering to her, the project had gone too far forward for her to back out gracefully. She decided that, once more, she'd just have to "bear up" and consoled herself with the thought that she probably wouldn't be able to hear my father anyway.

Positioned far enough from the edge that a sudden gust of wind or an attack of vertigo would not send her spiraling off into the canyon, but close enough that she could see down to the spot where he would be standing, my mother waited for my father to complete the hike and get into place. "Gooooo aheeeaaaad," he shouted up at her when he was ready. His voice easily leaped the distance between them, echoing a hundred times off the opposite wall of the canyon, each repetition of his words lapping against the next. She did not have time to analyze it, but the voice rising up out of the canyon was not the cold, sharp splinter she had expected. Still anticipating the passage of some dark shadow across her normally sunny disposition, however, she got in the pickup and started the engine, slowly releasing the clutch.

The vehicle jerked slightly but then rolled forward, although after ten feet or so, my mother happened to notice that the rope, rather than sliding out of sight over the rim, had gone slack and was bunching up beneath the bumper. Simultaneously, when she took her foot off the gas and let the motor idle, she thought she heard her name being called, so switching off the engine, she got out to see what had gone wrong, dreading once again the interchange she knew would ensue. When she leaned over the edge, she was startled and then amused to see the bag of cement resting on a rock ledge about three feet below her. She did not find the sight of my father cupping his hands around his mouth particularly amusing, however, and steeled herself for the assault on her ears.

But miraculously, the voice that wafted up to her was like the sighing of the wind through the cottonwoods, and yet she could hear it distinctly. As my father called up to her to lift the bag clear of the ledge and as she discussed with him the advisability of simply lowering it by hand—she was certainly strong enough to do that, she insisted—his voice seemed to belong to some laughing spirit of the canyon, and the canyon seemed a wonderful mechanism for amplifying and purifying sound.

As the rest of the cement went down—my mother put on her leather gloves and let the rope slide slowly through her hands—various and sundry problems came up, and my mother could see from the poses he struck that my father was getting into his windmilling mood. But his voice remained seductively full and mellow, and my mother found it so pleasing that occasionally she pretended not to hear him and called down to him to repeat what he had just told her. As the raising and lowering and tying and untying proceeded, therefore, my father's humor ripened, darkened, and then rotted entirely. He hollered louder and louder to vent his frustration, even as my mother smiled and began to whistle "This Ole House" in the intervals between her exchanges with him. Eventually, his voice gave out, as it always did, and he resorted to melodramatic flourishes of his hands, his arms, and his hat. From that point on, my mother began to feel that the job was getting tiresome, and that the sooner it was finished, the better. At last it was.

A couple of days after the pump house had been finished and my father was speaking to my mother again, he observed at breakfast that the gravity pump had not been worth all the trouble and that he supposed he just should have installed a windmill. My mother's hand, in the act of reaching for the salt, stopped in midair and then fluttered, empty, to the table as though it had been shot and wounded.

"Oh, Hart!" she exclaimed in a tone that sounded

similarly injured, "how could you say that? I *love* the gravity pump!" My father was taken aback by the strength of her objection to his criticism, though he had made it in hopes that she *would* object. Secretly, he liked the gravity pump, now that all the kinks had been worked out, but he thought that she thought it had been a bad idea.

"You like the pump?" he asked, astonished but hopeful.

"I really like the pump."

"It's not *that* good."

"It's amazing."

"You think?"

"I *do* think."

"How come?"

My mother hesitated a moment here. "Because it *sounds* so good," she finally said. "It sounds prettier than a windmill."

"Windmill hardly makes any sound a'tall."

"Yeah, but the pump makes *no* sound"

"You jus' said ya liked it because it made a pretty sound."

My mother smiled sweetly at him. "Silence sounds pretty sometimes . . . don't you think?"

My father was not sure how to take this last line but decided not to push my mother any further. Besides, he didn't care so much *why* she liked the pump as *that* she liked it. Anyway, he guessed he shouldn't be surprised that she was taken with it for other than practical reasons. "I reckin," he finally responded in a voice she found as pleasantly gentle as the wind rustling the leaves of the cottonwoods.

6   *Uncle John*

MY BROTHER TREY never openly questioned the truth of the Uncle John stories when my father told them, since he didn't want to hurt my father's feelings, but there came a day when he didn't enjoy them anymore the way my sister and mother and I still did. He'd shrug his shoulders and grin a little, but more out of politeness than pleasure. He appreciated as much as we did, however, the horror on my mother's face when my father spat in the iron skillet one day. Trey threw back his head and laughed long and infectiously like he had always used to, catching my mother around the waist and tickling her as he did so. Although she could stay angry at the rest of us for half a day at a time if she decided to, she could not resist my brother's good-natured teasing any more than anybody else could, and now it dispelled whatever reluctance she might have felt about joining in the general hilarity coming at her expense.

My father had spat in the skillet to see whether or not it was hot enough to fry round steak. To our earlier (though now comparatively less profound) amazement, he had suddenly taken my mother up on her "offer" to let him cook, since, as she put it, she apparently couldn't do it to suit him. Their feud, waged during the hour between chores and supper, had begun in jest, but fun sometimes has a way of turning sour, and now, my mother's usually sanguine temper flared up, though it stopped far short of serious anger. She was tired because she had had to fix a large dinner for the men who had helped us brand earlier in the day, and she was not very interested in cooking anything else, but we were all hungry and wanted chicken fried steak with gravy. My father, sitting at the kitchen table scanning the *Livestock Weekly* while she worked, had just said something mildly derogatory about the salad, a large bite of which he had eaten right off the serving spoon.

"Store passin' out free vinegar when ya shopped?" he asked without looking up from his paper. After banging the cold skillet down on the burner, my mother had invited him to step to the stove and take over, and then she had stood looking at him, her hands on her hips and tears gathering in her eyes, even though she pretended to be joking.

My father always felt bad when he hurt anybody's feelings. He was sensitive to our vulnerabilities but sometimes trod clumsily upon them, as you might blurt out some name you have sworn to repress all evening out of consideration for a guest to whom that name is hateful. We expected him to make up for his tactlessness, but we did not expect him to do so by cooking supper; in fact, his expression when he rose from his chair was neither sheepish nor contrite but mischievous instead, and so we waited in puzzled anticipation for his next move. My mother, a little taken aback by the swiftness with which he pushed his chair from the table, giggled tentatively and remained standing by the stove, so that when he spat and the foamy stuff sizzled in the pan—"reckin it's about ready," he said solemnly—she was close enough to grab the skillet out of his hand at the same time she shouted "Hart!"

"Don'cha want me ta cook?" he asked with mock innocence and surprise.

"Get out of here, you awful thing." My brother, sister, and I caught on a few seconds later.

After we had quieted down, my father, obviously pleased that he had pulled off his joke so successfully, recalled the time Uncle John had used this very strategy to avoid filling in for an injured camp cook during a roundup. None of the hands had been the least willing to discover what other culinary talents Uncle John might be hiding from them once he'd revealed his trick for testing a skillet. That tough cowboys had been so squeamish about a little spit probably had to do with the fact that Uncle John's had had tobacco in it. Fortunately, my father didn't chew.

None of us actually knew where the real Uncle John ended and the apocryphal Uncle John began. None of us much cared either, except my brother, who, at fifteen, had suddenly become intolerant of anything he considered idle or foolish, into which category he placed stories, especially ones that weren't strictly true. "Oh, he couldn't 'uv ridden that horse ten jumps if his life had depended on it," had been his dampening response to the raucous tale Paul Wayne had told during the branding that day about Ernest Ray, my sister's current love interest. The rest of us, with the exception perhaps of my sister, whose critical judgment was impaired when it came to Ernest Ray, had of course recognized the exaggeration of this particular detail, but we had embraced it willingly (if unconsciously) as an indispensable ingredient in the transformation of a simple report into a tale worth the telling.

Trey, however, was trying to trim off the fat. He wanted life lean, spare, and hard-hitting, so he had given up the extras. He had taken the feather and the beaded hatband off his Stetson, for example, and no longer sheared his horse's mane. Trey wanted the basics and the facts, and, as nobody knew precisely what these latter were with regard to Uncle John stories, he had little use for them.

One of the ironies of this attitude was that he, himself, was, or had been at least, a consummate storyteller; or rather, since he did not excel so much in the highly wrought gems of the true raconteur as in a kind of spicy gossip, he might more accurately have been called a color-commentator on the western scene. By the age of twelve, he had established a reputation as a "talker" and was especially known for his ability to work a Powder River squeeze chute (a cagelike contraption used in the branding or doctoring of large animals and requiring much precision in its operation), keep a running tally of the cattle going through the chute, and talk virtually nonstop to whoever happened to be in listening range. People got a kick out of the grown-up tone and cadences of his stories, but mostly they liked the stories themselves. They, together with the fact that he never missed catching an animal in the chute, made him a popular hand for the neighboring ranchers to hire, so that he was seldom short of spending money.

"Talked ta ol' B.J. yesterday," he'd begin. "Said him an' his buddy were truckin' some hawgs from Arizona ta Utah" (push up on the first long lever to release the animal's neck from the squeeze chute's yoke; push up on the second to widen the cage to normal size; prod the animal out of the chute through the now fully opened yoke; pull down on the third lever to open the back gate; pull down on the first, at just the right moment, to shut the yoke on the neck of the next animal entering the chute; pull down on the third to close the back gate; and finally, pull down on the second to squeeze the sides of the chute together so the animal can't struggle—"that's twenty-seven steers, thirty-nine heifers. Where's all those steers ya had, Hart? Looks like yer runnin' a dairy here"). "I guess ya cain't keep hawgs on the truck very long in this hot weather, so him an' ol' Doley were havin' ta run all night. Ol' Doley was drivin'" (push up on the first lever, push up on the second, prod the animal out, pull down on the third, pull down on the first, push up on the third, pull down on the second—"yeah, he's a steer but he's an ugly son of a gun. Where'd he come from? That's twenty-eight steers, thirty-nine heifers. Don' let 'em get his nose out there"). "Ol' Doley'd been drivin' all day and B.J., he'd jus' been sittin' watchin' the scenery go by. Donno what there is between Arizona an' Utah, but whatever it is, he'd been watchin' it. 'Bout ten o'clock that night, ol' Doley gets sleepy an' wants B.J. ta drive awhile. You know B.J., he don' really like ta drive that truck. Donno why he does it" (push, push, prod, pull, pull, push, pull; Trey swings like a monkey from one lever to the next. He is small and must use the weight of his body to engage the gears of the chute.

"That was twenty-nine steers, thirty-nine heifers. Ya'll are gonna confuse me with numbers like that"). "He tole me 'shoot, I didn't wanna drive 'at sucker all night.' He tole Doley, he said 'Doley, if you'll drive a couple three more hours, I'll take 'er the resta' the way in.' Doley said 'I'm too dern sleepy. You better drive. I'll get us all killed.' You know ol' Doley. He won't take a chance even if the raffle's free" (push, push, prod, pull, pull, push, pull; "hey there, cutie pie. Get yer leg outta the crack. Hold up a minute, we got a leg out here. Don' let 'er hurt herself. Twenty-nine steers, forty heifers"). "So ol' B.J. says 'well here. I got somethin'll cure that sleepy.' So he reaches down where Doley cain't see what he's doin' an' twists one a' the buttons off the cuff a' his shirt an' he says 'take this caffeine pill. It'll wake ya right up.' He said Doley popped that button in 'is mouth and swallowed hard. Said he was wide awake when they drove through Provo at nine the next mornin'" ("thirty steers, forty heifers").

"You know that ol' dun horse Vernon used ta have that he tried ta rope off of some? That ol' horse that got to rearin' straight up on 'is hind legs ever' time he rode 'em in the ropin' box? Ol' Souli Asa Shafer bought that horse an' tole Vernon he'd fix that rearin' up foolishness. Vernon was afraid he was gonna fall over backwards and kill somebody. So sure 'nuff, Souli Asa came an' got that horse th'other day. Now that boy . . . now that Souli Asa, he's a card. Vernon said he tol'em he got that ol' horse home an' the first time he tried ta rope some practice calves on 'em—I think he was gettin' ready ta go ta the rodeo in Flagstaff—th'ol' horse reared up. So Souli Asa went down an' bought himself a big balloon and filled it with warm water. Then he got a li'l ol' board an' drove a short nail all the way through one end ta where it'd barely stick out th'other side. Tied that balloon ta the headstall so it was layin' right between th'ol' horse's ears. Then when he rode in the ropin' box, he carried that li'l stick with 'em, and when th' horse reared up, he leaned forward an' smacked 'em between th' ears hard enough ta pop that balloon and prick the top a' his head. Vernon said Souli said that ol' horse jus' keeled over like he was dead almost before Souli could get 'is feet outta the stirrups an' get clear. Horse thought he felt his own blood runnin' down into his eyes and that he'd been killed. Like t'uv never gotten 'em ta stand back up, but he hasn't reared up since. Vernon says he'll make a whale of a ropin' horse. Wishes he hadn't sold 'em so cheap'' ("thirty-five steers, forty-two heifers'').

"Ol' Souli Asa, he's the same ol' boy trained his horse ta stop when he hollered at 'em by blindfoldin' 'em an' runnin' 'em at the barn. When he lacked a couple a' feet hittin' it, ol' Souli Asa jus' stepped off an' yelled 'whoa' at 'em. I don' know if he really did that. You cain't tell about that boy. You know what kinda talker he is" ("thirty-seven steers, forty-three heifers'').

The second irony of Trey not liking to waste his time on Uncle John was that, in a way, he was just like Uncle John. Uncle John was my father's great uncle and had lived on a little place across the creek from the ranch in the remote Big Bend area of West Texas on which my father had grown up. My father idolized him, not so much in the sense that he tried to emulate him—which was probably just as well, since Uncle John eventually drank his ranch away—as that he admired the singularly innovative approaches Uncle John took to solving the problems that life in such a place at such a time had to offer. Uncle John was what is known as an "original," though his was the wise and wily spirit one always imagines to have dwelled in any number of the men and women who settled the West. Of the Rogers boys, he took after Will more than Roy—although he was more a doer than a talker—and, in our family at least, he had the legendary status of the two of them combined. Whenever circumstances at the Heart-Diamond reminded my father of Uncle John, he'd tell a story. He did not hold Uncle John up to us as an example to induce us to work harder, rise earlier, or eat our greens, mainly because casting Uncle John's deeds into the genre of Sunday school lessons would have been difficult. Besides, he liked, as we did, precisely those traits that most smacked of mischief. We listened to the stories not because the hero of them was perfect but because he was not. He was a renegade, and he reassured us that we had a pint or two of unconventional blood coursing through our otherwise ordinary veins.

We knew it was true that, when he was twelve, Uncle John had been sent out into the little horse pasture to bring in the horses and had been gone two weeks instead of twenty minutes. The horses had recently been purchased from a ranch in the interior of Mexico and had decided to go home, to which spot Uncle John had tracked them (crossing the Rio Grande below Presidio) and from which he had brought them back. In his mature years, he had once yoked a wandering cow who refused to stay home on her own range to a gentle old burro who refused to leave the water lot in front of the house. Uncle John believed that the disappearance of both the cow and the burro had less to do with a flaw in his plan than with a flaw in the character of the burro. It was Uncle John who built a pen by planting hundreds of ocotillo cacti in a large circle, and Uncle John who first breached that formidable barrier to escape an enraged mama cow. He told my father all these tales himself, and he was not a man to lie outright unless he absolutely had to.

By the same token, we knew he had not been the first rancher in this mountainous and extremely rocky region of Texas to shoe his bulls, though he had, in fact, borrowed the idea when his registered Herefords, imported from back East, would not leave the corrals (which had been cleared of rocks) and go out in the pastures with the cows. He might have been the first person to medicate his own rattlesnake bite by cutting it open and filling it with salt, though of course necessity was the true mother of this invention, no doctor having as yet ventured into the territory. Still, Uncle John wasn't sure but what he'd heard about this cure from somebody else and refused to take credit for it.

It was harder to tell with other stories that got told about Uncle John, but as I say, whether they really happened or not did not matter much to anybody except Trey, the one who should have had the greatest affinity for them by virtue of his resemblance to their hero. For Trey, like Uncle John, was a person other people liked to be around and work with. There was never any telling what Uncle John would do next (though everyone liked to tell about what he *had* done). Likewise, there was never any telling what Trey would say next.

In fact, however, Trey wasn't saying much. He no longer told stories around the squeeze chute or the branding pen because he was trying to be reserved and self-possessed—trying to be the kind of man who kept his thoughts to himself, but about whom everybody knew that, were he to utter them, they'd be the thoughtiest thoughts ever expressed on the subject, whatever it was.

The TV showing of "Shane" had precipitated the metamorphosis of Trey's personality, though perhaps we all go through periods when we want to be taken more seriously. Shane, with his solid stance, dangerous eyes, and silent ways, was the stereotypical cowboy. You respected him and you didn't mess with him. This was the enviously tidy relationship with his fellow humans that my brother was now trying to cultivate, even though real cowboys generally hold even empty conversation in higher regard than silence (however charged it might be with meaning), in the presence of which they tend to toe the ground and spit more often than usual. My brother never articulated his new philosophy—doing so would have required him to talk, of course—but I had watched the movie with him and had noticed the changes in his behavior shortly thereafter. Our resolutions to reshape our personalities are normally short-lived, as we usually decide we aren't so bad after all, but the new Trey had been with us since summer. When occasionally caught off guard, he allowed the real person to resurface, but he wasn't much fun anymore. Neighbors who had never hesitated before to help us brand or fix a fence when we asked them were beginning to find excuses.

At about this time, two of Trey's friends, brothers from a nearby ranch who had not entirely given up on him, came out to the Heart-Diamond to help him ride the Middle Pasture and check on the cattle. He occasionally visited their ranch and kept them company while they rode their extensive pipeline system to look for leaks, and, in former days at least, he had relieved for them much of the tedium of that task. But now it seemed to them he was beginning to contribute to it. They were a lively pair who were always breaking bones, wrecking pickups, and chasing "women."

On this particular afternoon, the three boys rode by the windmill and found, slobbering and gasping for air, a Charolais bull who evidently had something hung in his throat—a prickly pear thorn perhaps or a twig of mesquite. His tongue was swollen and protruded slightly, and from the looks of him, he hadn't eaten or drunk for a couple of days. The boys eased him into the big pen at the windmill with the intention of riding back to get the pickup and trailer so they could haul him to the house and run him in the squeeze chute. He was not going to appreciate their ministrations, they knew, regardless of the fact that he'd probably starve to death without them.

"Aw let's jus' head 'n heel 'em here," Wes, the youngest of the three proposed. "I got me a date tonight. Haulin' 'em in'll take forever." Wes always liked the shortest, most entertaining route to the completion of any chore.

"Better not," Trey replied, eyeing the bull, who eyed him back. "Might jerk a horse down."

"Me an' Ken'll rope 'em. We rope on these horses all the time. They won't get jerked down. Besides, he looks too weak ta fight."

"You know better'n that," Trey told him—which of course he did.

That roping the bull was a brash and potentially dangerous thing to do only whetted Wes's appetite, however, so he kept on. He was large and bullishly strong himself and did not yet appreciate that his flesh was heir to a thousand natural shocks or that he might profitably hesitate before taking up arms to oppose a sea of troubles. He was, in short, no Hamlet, nor would anybody looking at him have mistaken him for that meditative young man. Trey, furthermore, whose better judgment struggled quite vigorously for awhile, finally allowed it to be overcome by an image. In his mind's eye he saw himself and Ken skillfully heading and heeling the bull, removing the thorn from his throat, and then—and this was the most seductive part of his scenario—recoiling their ropes with that supremely confident but understated motion of the winning gunfighter blowing the smoke away from the nose of his .45, his eyes glowing a technicolor green. "In the ol' days before there were squeeze chutes," he reasoned with himself, "they'd 'uv jus' roped 'em."

Before too long he was shaking out a heading loop. Wes protested vigorously that the idea was his and that he should get to rope, but he was not inclined to dispute Trey's point that Wes himself was the only one strong enough to tail the bull down once the ropes were on him. Ken, who had always been the quietest of the three until Trey's Shane phase, unwound the carrying strap from his nylon rope, his lips taut either with excitement or anxiety.

As it happened, the bull was in no mood to be trifled with. Two days without food and water had not improved his already less-than-sugary disposition, and he stood in one corner of the pen glowering at the pesky intruders into his domain, every now and then pawing the white caliche dirt so that clouds of it billowed up around his not-so-terribly long but plenty-long-enough horns. Riding slowly toward him, Trey observed uneasily the breadth of the glossy white back, the depth of the chest, and the musculature of the hind quarters. The bull was not particularly tall, but he was impressively solid, and Trey had an inkling now why the machines they use to remove large impediments are called bulldozers. He knew before he ever took the first swing that roping Marmaduke—for that was the bull's name—was going to be a big mistake, but he could not back out now for obvious reasons. Wes, sitting on the fence until such time as the bull could be safely caught, grinned eagerly.

Trey had imagined himself lining the bull out in a lope across the pens, standing up in his stirrups, and zinging one of those smart little rodeo arena loops around his "rack." Strangely, however, the white bull did not move at all when the horse approached, except to work his tongue and raise his head, so Trey just draped a sloppy "pen" loop around the widely splayed horns, easy targets now that the bull had thrust them defiantly forward. Then he jerked his slack and dallied the end of the rope around his saddle horn, bracing himself for the jarring impact of Marmaduke's first plunge, and prepared to unwrap the rope at the first sign that his horse could not hold the weight.

But, in fact, the bull only snorted, took a couple of steps forward, and then stood still again, waiting. He seemed to be calculating the odds. In some respects, this was far more unnerving than his fighting the rope would have been. Neither was Ken, a heeler of such talent that he had roped steers in professional rodeos even as a small boy, able to throw his "money-winner" nor display the incredible adroitness with which, after a catch, he could dally the rope before it was ripped fiercely through his hands by the running steer. Since Marmaduke was not running or even walking, Ken had to resort to the workmanlike expedient of laying a trap—that is, he had to throw his loop beneath the bull in such a way that, remaining open, it leaned against the front of the hind legs, a gaping snare waiting for its victim to move forward an inch or two. Such a loop was no mean feat, but, as the slow-motion version of a rodeo catch, it was not beyond the capacity of the average cowboy and certainly not the snappy retort to his own crackling catch that Trey had envisioned.

Now it was up to Trey to drag the bull forward into the heel trap. He hoped that either Marmaduke didn't weigh as much as he appeared to, or that the sorrel horse he was riding was stronger than usual. He did not relish the prospect of breaking in on whatever thoughts were concentrating in the massive white brow, but, keeping the rope tight, he turned his horse's tail to the bull and clicked his tongue, the cue to the horse to pull. The sorrel leaned into the rope, and then, as Marmaduke didn't budge, crouched down almost on his knees, scrabbling in the dust that covered the hardpan underneath for a grip. The veins popped out on his neck and the rope began to stretch. But still Marmaduke didn't move, even though for a moment, in fact, it seemed to Trey that he could hear a scraping sound, as though the horse's sharp hooves were losing their hold and being dragged backwards over the chalky blackboard floor of the pen.

Just as the beeswax that had been worked into the nylon rope to keep it pliant began to melt and run down the saddle horn (or so Trey said), Marmaduke crow-hopped forward one step to relieve the pressure on his horns. The sorrel tilted up on his nose and almost knocked out a front tooth, but he got his balance and lunged to take up the slack. Simultaneously, Ken jerked his rope tight around the hind legs, and Marmaduke was "caught," although the casual spectator might have had difficulty determining just who had whom in the resultant tableau. Both horses, Ken's backing up and Trey's continuing to lean forward, pulled mightily on their respective ropes, trying to drag the bull's hind feet out from under him. For a minute or two Marmaduke stood firm, but when Wes, who had jumped down into the pen the moment both ropes were on the bull, began to pull sideways on his tail, he slowly, almost gently, toppled over in a puff of caliche dust.

Wes kneeled, planting one knee firmly on the bull's neck and the other against his back. Leaning across the mountainous shoulder, he grasped the right foreleg just below the middle joint, bent the leg double, and pulled it hard enough back toward the shoulder to tilt the bull slightly up on his back, thus keeping the bottom foreleg sufficiently off the ground to prevent the bull from getting any purchase with it. As long as Marmaduke stayed in this position—stretched out between two sweating horses with Wes holding the free foreleg—he presumably could do little damage.

But in fact it was eerie how little damage Marmaduke seemed disposed to do. His resistance to being thrown had amounted only to his having rooted himself as firmly as he could to the spot on which he had stood. He did not fling himself about or bellow or charge the horses. He only stared, unblinkingly it seemed to Trey, first at one boy and then at another, as though he were deciding which of them was the weak link in the chain that bound him.

"I shoulda known better," Trey admitted later, "but really, of all the wrecks that coulda happened, I cain't believe which one *did* happen. After we threw 'em, I tied my rope solid and turned ol' Safety Pin back around. Then I got off an' tied my reins ta the rope so he'd stay facin'. He knew what he was s'posed ta do an' kept the rope tight. Ol' Wes was haulin' back on th'ol' bull's front leg, an' I had my hand crammed down 'is throat pullin' mesquite brush outta his tongue. If th'ol' bull had wanted to, he coulda flicked 'is leg and jerked Wes clear over 'is belly, but he didn't do anything 'cept lay there figgerin' out how he was gonna kill all three of us. He bellered real low once, an' Wes kep' sayin' 'look how this thing's lookin' at me. 'Je ever see one lay still an' look atcha like that? Gives me the creeps.' An' ya know that ol' bull . . . he really was givin' us th' eye of death, jus' layin' there real quiet waitin' for his chance.

"Anyway, we still prob'ly wouldn'a had any problem if we hadn'a had problems. Ken coulda jus' kep' 'is hind legs drug out from under 'em long enough for me ta take the head rope off an' for me'n Wes ta get someplace safe. Then Ken woulda jus' spurred up an' pitched 'em some slack. The heel rope 'ud come off by itself as soon as the bull pulled it open. But instead, I had my hand down 'is throat an' ol' Wes, he kep' askin' me if I'd ever seen 'Jaws.' You know ol' Wes, he's not scared a' much, but I could see he wasn't jus' teasin' me. He was gettin' pretty durn nervous 'bout that bull gettin' up with him out there 'n the middle a' the pen. He was a pretty good ways from the fence.

"Then when we were 'bout finished, things started ta happen. Ol' Safety Pin was practic'ly sittin' down, but he was half asleep by now since the bull hadn' ever moved. All of a sudden a durned li'l ol' whirlwind came along and blew Wes's hat off the fence post where he'd hung it. Donno why he'd taken it off 'cept I guess it was kinda new. It was black an' he prob'ly didn' wanna get that white dust all over it. Cain't get that stuff out with anything 'cept those high-powered vacuum cleaners they have down at the car wash, but we tried that with somebody's hat one time an' it sucked the crown all outta shape. Anyway, the hat blew smack up against Safety Pin's flank an' kinda stuck there like a colt tryin' ta nurse. Safety Pin decided he better stampede while he had an excuse, so while he was dancin' around gettin' ready ta do that, he gave me enough slack ta jerk the head rope off. Havin' a scared horse tied to a rope tied to a bull fixin' ta get up seemed more dangerous ta me at the time than jus' the bull, who I figgered Ken 'ud hold long enough for us ta run.

"But when he saw ol' Safety Pin startin' toward 'em, that ol' bull started strugglin'. Ol' Ken, he was 'bout half asleep too an' he'd let 'is horse slack off jus' enough for the bull ta get 'is legs part way out. Ken yanked 'is horse back, but the rope drew up around the bull's hooves and was slippin' off fast. I started hollerin' at Wes ta run. At first he couldn't let go. He kinda froze up an' 'is mouth was hangin' open. Wisht I'd had me a camera. Then he let go an' I mean he *boogied* across that pen. You know he's kinda bowlegged and cain't outrun a hobbled duck, but he jus' knew that ol' bull was breathin' down 'is neck. Boy, I wisht I'd had me a camera. So what does he do but he runs ta the nearest thing he can climb which happens ta be *my* horse. Safety Pin had decided he was too tired ta waste a lotta energy gettin' scared. Wes's hat had kinda come unclamped an' fallen under 'is feet, so he tromped on it two or three times tryin' ta get away from it, but then he jus' went back ta sleep. Boy he came to when Wes hit the saddle though. But that kinda left me out in the water with no life jacket. Ol' Ken, he was tryin' ta save me, but 'bout that time, his rope popped off th'ol' bull's toes."

"So whaja do?" my sister asked, grinning expectantly. Obviously, he'd done something, for he had lived to tell the tale.

"So when I saw th'ol' bull knew he was loose an' was fixin' ta find 'is feet—ya know how those big-bellied ones haveta kinda roll around sometimes ta get up—while he was doin' that, I figgered kinda brisk that he could get up an' outrun me ta the fence, so I was headin' for Safety Pin. But then I saw Wes sittin' in the middle a' *him*, so I stopped an' stood there like a' idiot for about thirty minutes. I looked at Wes an' then I looked at the bull—don' know which one I hated the most right then—and then I looked at the fence. It was so far over there I couldn't tell how many strands a' wire it had in it. So then I figgered there was only one thing I could do. I started runnin' back toward that ol' bull an' got to 'em jus' as he was gettin' up. I reached down an' grabbed me a handful a' dirt an' I threw it right in 'is eye. Couldn't get ta th' other eye, but I figgered one eyeful might keep 'em busy enough for a minute. Kinda distract 'em ya know. Then I figgered I'd better run from 'is blind side. Fence was further that way, but if he'd spotted me, he'd a' been twice as mad. Cleared that six-foot fence by a foot and a half and kep' runnin'. Finally tripped over a root an' my life flashed through my mind, but when I looked back over my shoulder, that ol' bull was jus' standin' there in the pen shakin' 'is head an' battin' 'is eye. After awhile, I jus' strolled over easy-like an' opened the gate, an' when he got 'is eye cleared out, he trotted back ta 'is cows. Decided not ta mess with me anymore."

"Pretty good figurin," my sister said, "and lots of it too. How'd ya ever think a' that little trick?"

"Uncle John did it once," Trey replied, tilting his chair

back from the supper table and sticking a toothpick in his mouth. "Only he did it to an ol' longhorn cow, an' I think he spit chewin' tabacca in both 'er eyes before she ever got up."

We had Trey back.

7   *The Wild Heifer*

THE WILD HEIFER HAD BEEN IN LABOR for three hours and had made no progress beyond pushing out two tiny hooves and forelegs. She, herself, was tiny and fine-boned like a deer, and Ernest, my sister's husband, had predicted she'd have difficulties, especially because this was her first calf. He had brought her to the house and put her in the corral a week or so before "to keep an eye on her." But naturally, Ernest wasn't at the house today. He hardly ever was. He was a "troubleshooter" for Mr. Dunn, a man who owned three ranches in the area, one of which was currently suffering the ill effects of a broken windmill. Ernest had gone "to see about it," thoughtlessly taking with him the eyes that figured so prominently in his parlance and with which he had intended to monitor these final critical stages of the heifer's pregnancy. My sister had been walking down the hill to the corral every twenty minutes or so to keep *her* eye on the heifer and was beginning to realize that she'd probably have to help deliver the calf.

She wished she had studied more than two semesters of animal science, as she had planned to when she first went off to New Mexico State and enrolled in the pre-vet program. But she had met Ernest, quiet, red-haired, and movie-star handsome, in her sophomore year. He, too, had been raised on a ranch and wanted to ranch after he graduated. She wanted to be with him and figured she'd have plenty of chances to doctor on animals if she were going to be a rancher's wife. So she had switched her major to foreign languages, thinking that fluency in Spanish might come in handy for their business someday because somewhere around forty percent of the population of the state spoke it. "Maybe I should try conjugating 'to give birth to' three times," she thought disgustedly to herself. The film she had seen in her last animal science class about delivering colts wasn't going to be much help either. It had advised calling the vet and keeping the mare's "environment" clean. She had no telephone, and she imagined that the heifer would neither lie cooperatively on a pile of fresh straw nor allow herself to be bathed with warm water and swaddled in gauze. So far, the waspy creature had leapt up, protruding forelegs notwithstanding, and bolted to the far corner of the pen each time she had caught sight of my sister. She'd probably have to be roped and tied down to be helped.

But Flee (my sister's nickname, a contraction of her given name, Frances Lee) did have some credentials which justified her basic confidence that she could manage this problem. She and Ernest had been married about six months, during which time Ernest had worked for Mr.

Dunn. Or rather, a perpetually self-renewing fund of burst pipes, stray cows, sick horses, and flat tires had meant that they both had worked, and, although only Ernest received a wage, Flee could handle many of the jobs he was assigned to do and was the main reason he could keep up with all the trouble three ranches dished out. She had just spent a good two months, furthermore, nursing Mr. Dunn's favorite horse back to health after he nearly cut his leg off on a barbed wire fence, and she had earned much praise, if no profit, from the boss, whose shrewdness in getting two cowboys for the price of one was gradually dawning on him.

Flee did not mind not getting paid. She loved the life she led, and she loved the way the southwestern mountains sliced cleanly through the sky. She and Ernest dreamed of owning fifty sections of this country someday. Ernest was good at figuring angles and cutting corners just where they needed to be cut—good at the geometry of ranching, in other words—and was bound to be successful if he got a few breaks. He tended toward "workaholism," but Flee admired horses and people possessed of this trait. To her, it was indicative of a more general quality that she considered indispensable to a well-formed character and that she referred to as "try." Ernest had lots of "try." So did Mr. Dunn, a wealthy man who had come to ranching from the city, and who, to most people's amazement, was doing pretty well at it. But Flee perhaps had more "try" than anybody. Although she had never actually "pulled" a calf, she had watched our parents do it several times and was not the least daunted by the prospect. In fact, she looked forward to the challenge of singlehandedly saving the life of the wild heifer and her baby. What might Mr. Dunn say to that?

Pluck was not all that Flee brought to this situation, even though it was her favorite virtue and the one to whose practices she attributed her other assets and skills—her "know how." Growing up on the Heart-Diamond, she had had ample opportunity to learn to do many things, and she had learned to do them very well, largely, she believed, because of her unflappable conviction that she could accomplish anything she set her mind to. Our mother accused her once of taking too literally and too much to heart the *Bookhouse Books* version of "The Little Engine That Could," but it is always difficult to argue with success, and my sister had lots of it on her side. She had been an "A" student in high school and college, for example, and a top rider on New Mexico State's rodeo team. She was one of the best branding pen ropers in the county, never getting rattled, as the men frequently did, by branding pen "humor"—the merciless thrust of which was always that the hand doing the "cush" job of roping should relinquish it to the greater talents of the hand doing the dirty work on the ground (and the teasing, of course). To a ragged chorus of such "discouraging words" and armed with confidence, she would ride into the bunch of calves wadded up in the corner of the pen, select an unbranded one, and flick a loop under his belly. "Aw, Leatherwood," she'd say as the calf's back heels fell into the loop just like they were supposed to (she called the men by their last names as they did each other; they called her Flee), "you know ya gotta leave this high-tech stuff ta somebody with lotsa fine tunin' in her wrists and fingers. Soon as ya learn ta give that blackleg vaccine shot ta those calves without drawin' blood, I might let'cha heel at one."

"I swear, that Flee jus' don' hardly miss them heelin' loops," one of the men would say wonderingly to another as they flanked yet another of her catches, his tone conveying, besides admiration, a wistful desire that she would miss now and then so he could "breathe a spell."

She had a knack for "healing" as well as for "heeling," which had been the basis of her earlier intentions to be a vet and which she also attributed to the power of positive thinking. Mr. Dunn's horse had been only the most recent of a long line of beneficiaries of her care.

"I'm not sure there's much sense puttin' a lot a' time in on 'em," Mr. Dunn had said when Flee heard about the horse and volunteered to "doctor on 'em some."

"Big muscle right at the top a' his front left leg is cut plumb in two and jus' kinda sticks out. Vet says he cain't sew it up 'cause it'll jus' rip out every time th'ol' horse moves."

"Guess he prob'ly won't get any better if nobody does anything for 'em," my sister had suggested. "Won't cost anything ta try 'cept a bottle a' barb wire liniment."

"Reckin I can swing that," Mr. Dunn had assented finally, "if tendin' 'em don' put'cha out any." He had trailered the horse over the next day.

The wound, one of the worst Flee had ever seen, had been dirty and caked with blood. For the first two days, she had had to hobble the horse, a long-bodied, well-bred bay, to keep him still while she cleaned out the proud flesh and poured medicine into the gaping hole. Although these twice-daily ministrations obviously hurt him, he seemed finally to comprehend, as dogs sometimes do when you're pulling porcupine quills out of their muzzles, that the stinging pain was necessary. Afterward, he'd only flinch and drop his nose on her bent head, as if to remind her to be careful. Mr. Dunn called him "Rebel," but she called him "Chueco" ("Crippled" or "Crooked"). After the severed muscle had begun to knit itself back together, she led him two or three miles every day to keep it from bunching up into a knotty scar. In two months' time, the wound had nearly closed (even though the two ragged ends of the muscle had not matched up evenly), and Flee watched proudly as Chueco trotted and bucked around the pen. "I'll be durned," Mr. Dunn had said the first time he saw the horse walk without limping, "how'd ya do that?"

"You just gotta talk ta those cuts kinda like ya talk ta plants ta make 'em grow. They'll just close right up."

"I'll be durned," Mr. Dunn had said again, uncertain as to how much stock Flee actually put in the medicinal value of words to wounds.

Now when my sister went to check on her, the heifer moaned in pain but still got up and moved nervously away. She wobbled horribly and seemed on the verge of collapsing. She had probably not seen many human beings in her two brief years of life on this large ranch and did not like the idea of one of them intruding on what nature and instinct told her should be a private affair. Nevertheless, in forty-five minutes, she had managed to expel only an inch or two more of foreleg. If she were not better provided for than nature was managing to do, her calf would suffocate, and she would probably die of shock. She watched my sister warily as the pain forced her to lie down again; her body went rigid as the wave of a contraction rolled through it.

Flee glanced at her watch and then at a point on the horizon twenty-five miles away where the dirt road leaving her front yard disappeared over a saddleback between two tall mesas. If Ernest's pickup were on that road anywhere between the house and the mesas, it would whirl up into the otherwise spotless atmosphere an easily visible cloud of dust. But there was no sign of the pickup, and Flee headed for the barn to get some ropes: a good nylon with which to catch the heifer, an old "true-blue manila" to tie around her hind legs, and a soft cotton with which to pull the unborn calf if that turned out to be necessary.

An orderly birth introduces the calf's forelegs first and next his head, tucked neatly between his legs as though he were a diver entering the water. Since the heifer had gotten through the first stage a while back, it was likely that the baby calf's head was peering over its shoulder and would have to be straightened, after which the birth might possibly proceed normally. My sister would have to force her hand through the birth canal and into the womb, grope around that warm, damp, compartment until she found the calf's nose, and then draw the head forward.

The first trick, however, would be to "immobilize" the patient, who, amazingly, stood up yet again when Flee climbed off the fence into the pen, ropes in hand. The heifer did not move, however, but only glared and pawed the ground threateningly, as she would have done had a coyote or a mountain lion disturbed her out in the pasture. Flee paused to see what the heifer had in mind to do and then slowly advanced toward her. The heifer seemed to have forgotten for the time being that she was in the throes of labor and eyed fiercely the approaching "varmint," tossing up her head as she considered whether to give way to her terror or to her anger. She did neither but stood her ground tremblingly until the loop settled around her horns.

Its touch seemed to trigger the thousand tight springs inside her, and she charged her antagonist, though in two or three strides the charge had receded to a weak-kneed trot. My sister, anticipating it, made her own charge toward the side of the corral, yanking the loop tight around the base of the horns as she turned to run. She was careful, for the duration of the comically ill-matched footrace that ensued, not to drop her end of the rope, and, after she scrambled over the fence a good three yards ahead of the heifer, she dallied it twice around the top of one of the railroad ties to which the fence boards were nailed. When the heifer stopped just short of the fence and set back on the rope, Flee set back on it too, using her weight to keep it from slipping through the wraps on the post; when the heifer stepped toward the fence to snuff a warning at her captor, that misunderstood Samaritan tightened the resultant slack and thus drew the heifer's horned head tightly up against the fence; and when at last the exhausted victim of the labor pains and the chase began to slump, my sister fed her sufficient rope that she could lower her head to the ground along with the rest of her body.

When it seemed that the heifer was too weak to move for a few minutes, Flee unwound the rope from the top of the railroad tie and snubbed the heifer's head securely to the bottom of it. "Now, cow," she said as she viewed with much satisfaction the prostrate form, "why don'cha let me help ya help yerself?" to which rhetorical question the heifer replied with shallow pants. She strained magnificently with the next contraction, stretching out her neck in her agony and her effort until most of her head was shoved beneath the fence, but she produced nothing more than a thin trickle of fluids and blood, which fell into the dust under her tail. Flee used a square steer roping knot to tie up her hind legs.

Lying on her stomach with her blond hair trailing in

the dirt and blood and with her nose unpleasantly close to a fresh pile of bright green manure, Flee tried to contort her own body in such a way that the heifer's struggles would not dislocate her arm. That venturesome member was now up to its shoulder in "heifer," and its fingers tentatively touched the body of the calf, trying to determine in what awkward posture the gangly youngster had decided to present itself to the world. Several times, she had been afraid her arm was about to be pulled from its socket, but she was reluctant to withdraw it because getting it in there had been so strenuous and tiring. When she did have to retract it part way, she could see that it was flecked with gobbets of dark blood. Her cotton shirt, wet and sticky, clung to her back, accentuating the prominent blades of her strong shoulders. Her own breath came now in short gasps between the longer groans she emitted as, with tremendous effort, she maneuvered her cramped hand around the restrictive quarters of the heifer's womb. "What're ya doin' in there, ya little stinker?" she murmured and then held her breath so she could "hear" better what her fingers, tentatively poking and prodding, were "saying" to her. She was trying to be as gentle as the brutal conditions would allow, though she doubted that the heifer could appreciate anymore the distinction between a sensitive hand and a careless one.

   Suddenly, my sister's exploring fingers found an ear, and when they then traced the outline of the head and the curvature of the neck, she could tell that sure enough, the baby's head was folded back against its shoulder. Having made that discovery, she allowed herself to pause and relax her stiffening muscles, resting her cheek momentarily against her free arm. There was no shade in the barren pen in which she and the heifer lay except for the narrow strips of shadow cast by the fence rails, one of which fell across the heifer's eyes. "Maybe she believes she's under a tree," Flee thought to herself. She had begun to hope that there was for the heifer, however ephemeral, some twilight bands of comfort relieving intermittently the white heat of her pain.

To get at the calf's nose, Flee had to fish with the tips of her fingers. She barely had any feeling left in them anymore and would like to have removed her arm for a little while to restore its circulation and to breathe a spell, but she knew the heifer had been in labor too long and that the calf was bound to be in distress by now. She groped along the top of the head, brushing once against the other ear. The afternoon was perfectly calm, and she heard no sounds. Once, her attention strangely detached itself from the life-and-death struggle that had absorbed it so completely for the last half hour and settled on a sparrow sitting on the edge of the water trough in the opposite corner of the pen. The bird was singing, and my sister lingered there long enough to soak in some of its bright busy cry.

She wanted to listen a second or two more, but she was abruptly summoned back to the difficult business of saving the calf when her fingers curled around its nose and jaws. As the heifer twitched and sighed deeply, rattling the air through her nostrils, Flee pulled cautiously on the little head, not knowing how much tension either it or the heifer could safely withstand. Nothing gave, however, so she pulled harder. Still nothing gave. The heifer lay quietly, semiconscious, her eyes rolled far back into her head. She was simply enduring the contractions now, too exhausted to exert herself. As my sister tugged more insistently on the baby calf's unbudging head, she was astonished to discover herself on the verge of tears. She gritted her teeth, trying to absorb the lump in her chest, and concentrated hard on the tips of her fingers—observing through them that mysterious dark world that seemed bent on ending the very life it had nourished for nine months. "This is ridiculous," Flee thought, including in her opprobrium both her tears and the perversity of nature. "Wish I could stick my head in there an' see what's goin' on." A wry grimace had just wrinkled the skin on her chin when, with the same degree of resistance a door offers when you close it against a storm, the calf's nose came around. "Aw right!" Flee shouted out loud, wasting no time withdrawing her arm. "I knew we could do it!"

She worked rapidly now, and more confidently, looping the cotton rope around the exposed front legs. She had to get the calf out immediately, so she pulled hard on the rope. "Okay little cow," she addressed the heifer, "you have ta try a little now. Don't just lay here an' let yer baby die." The shadow that, earlier, had screened the heifer's eyes from the sun, now fell like a yoke across her glossy red neck. She did not stir for the first minute or two that my sister pulled, though a small wedge of brown could now be seen in the corner of her eye. Flee spoke more sharply to her. "If ya don't wanna be hamburger meat for the buzzards, ya better get with the program, cow." Whether in response to this dire portrait of her future or because she sensed that her efforts might now be rewarded, the heifer suddenly strained, and a head, covered with a filmy membrane, came slipping into view. With several more heaves, the heifer delivered the rest of her baby in a gush of blood and afterbirth. "Welcome ta the great Southwest," my sister greeted the red-and-white newcomer. "Hope ya like it here."

But it was only a moment before she saw that the calf was not breathing. She hurriedly cleaned the membrane from its nose and pressed on its ribs to start its lungs. "Come on, little feller," she urged, "you can make it." She had seen other calves born "dead" who only needed some encouragement before, with a frightful convulsion, they sucked in a first great draught of air. The heifer tried to raise her head but was too weak to fight the rope that held her. Flee paid her no heed, but hammered, more roughly now, on the calf's ribs, which stuck up beneath the wet skin. When the little animal still did not breathe, she picked it up by its hind legs, as she had once seen a vet do, and dropped it on the ground, hoping to jar the heart and lungs into life. Even as she worked to revive the baby, she was awed by its fragile beauty. Its hooves were shiny yellow and its delicate, almost transparent ears, pressed against its head, accentuated the helplessness of the wide eyes. My sister punched down savagely on the rib cage again and then opened the mouth to clean it out. Only when she saw how the gaping mouth transformed the naive baby face into a hideous mask of death did she leave the calf alone. She noticed, standing back with her hands on her hips and gazing down at the carcass, how the flank caved in to expose the pelvic bone and how the swollen tongue protruded. The calf had probably been dead for quite some time. Walking to the fence, my sister squatted in the dirt and rested her head on a board.

She roused herself five minutes later when the heifer became restless. It occasionally happens that, in passing through the birth canal of a particularly small-framed cow, the calf will squeeze, and thus paralyze, the large nerve carrying stimuli along the cow's spine to her back legs. The heifer needed to be gotten up as soon as possible to "awaken" the nerve if it were only traumatized and to be convinced that she, as well as her nerve, was still in the land of the living. Sometimes, my sister knew, cows just gave up. "Sometimes," she said to herself, "I don't blame 'em."

"Not yet though," she warned the wild heifer as she untied her legs and removed the rope from around her horns. The heifer's body had, through the force of my sister's pulling on the unborn calf, been stretched out as far as the rope had permitted it to be stretched, as though she had been tortured on the rack and not yet released from it. But her eyes had rolled back around into their proper places, even though they did not seem focused on anything in particular. In a moment, unless she had already decided there was no sense prolonging her misery or unless she were actually paralyzed, she'd try to stand. Flee prepared to assist her, grasping her tail, the only appendage upon which she could get any purchase. It was still slimy with blood, and a thick rope of afterbirth trailed out of the vulva. "Yer a mess," my sister informed her.

The heifer began by trying to bring her back legs under control. Horses raise themselves from a prone position by rolling up on their "honkers" (getting their knees under them) and then using their front legs to pull themselves up. Cows, once they are resting on their knees, must stand their back legs up first, and from this awkward position, get their front legs straightened out and into operation. The heifer had sat up shortly after she had been untied, a sign that she intended at least to try to walk again, but clearly, the difficult and prolonged delivery had injured her. She could get her rear end hoisted into the air, but her back legs were too rubbery to support her body for more than a few seconds and buckled beneath her each time she tried to shift her weight off her front knees enough to unbend them. She would scrabble in the dirt, plowing a furrow with her chin, before collapsing with a grunt. She had feeling in her back legs, however, and they seemed to be getting gradually more responsive to the commands she was giving them.

"You can get up, dumb brain," Flee urged her. "Yer legs are only asleep." When the tough tone seemed to fall on deaf ears—the heifer was still on her knees but was not struggling anymore—she adopted a gentler one. "Come on, little cow beast," she coaxed, "there's not enough of ya ta feed a good-sized buzzard anyway. If ya die, you'll smell up the pen. Get up." The heifer turned her head and glared. "Well, if ya don't want me pullin' on yer tail, ya can just do somethin' about it." She lightly toed the heifer's thigh with her boot and then kicked her harder and twisted her tail. "Get up, nit wit. Don't quit on me now." With the same unpredictable and swift summoning of strength with which she had given birth to the dead calf, the heifer brought her unruly legs to order, straightened the bent ankles, scrambled to her front feet, swayed briefly, and then, in a shaky walk, pursued my laughing sister across the pen to the fence before returning to smell her dead baby.

When Ernest finally got home that night, Flee told him what had happened. Exhausted and covered with windmill grease, he asked her to pull his boots off and fix him a glass of iced tea. Then he said, not unkindly, "You might shoulda started helpin' her a little sooner." He sipped the tea. "Prob'ly couldn't a' done much else fer the calf though."

"You think we better keep her around for a couple a' days 'til she's stronger?" my sister asked him as she watched him drink. "She's still a little wobbly. Feed might help 'er a little." They were seated at the kitchen table, over which hung the only light burning in the house.

"I imagine Mr. Dunn'll want me ta haul 'er ta the sale Monday, since she's not gonna have a calf ta raise. I got three 'r four head I gotta take."

"You really think he will?" Flee inquired quietly. "It was just her first baby."

"Not much sense keepin' 'er, I don't suppose," Ernest replied. "She cain't make 'em any money standin' aroun' eatin' and not feedin' a calf."

"Can'cha tell 'em ya think she'll make a good cow? She's an awful good heifer and he cares what you think."

"You know as well as I do it'd be safer ta sell 'er. She might not ever really get over bein' crippled." Flee was not sure she could say right then *what* she knew.

A week after the heifer had been sold, Mr. Dunn drove up the narrow dirt road. For forty-five minutes or more, Flee could glance out her kitchen window and track his slow progress by watching his dust. He grinned at her through the open window of the pickup when he finally arrived and then shouted, "Hey, come over here an' see what I got." His sunburned cheeks creased in folds when he smiled. "Lookahere." He jerked his chin back over his shoulder to point. In the bed of the pickup lay a thin mountain lioness and her two cubs. All three animals had been shot through the head. "Men got these suckers up by the white tank on the mountain. Guess she was bringin' 'er babies in ta water. Good thing we got 'em before they grew up enough ta cause trouble."

Flee stared at the bodies. A soft breeze ruffled the cubs' baby fur but did nothing to soften the rigid attitude of death in which they lay. The mother's old yellow eyes stared vacantly at the mountains in the distance and her ribs showed through her mangy hide. "Yeah, looks like they were a real menace," Flee answered after awhile, and then saying nothing more turned on her heel and strode to the house. Through angry tears, she groped for the door handle. Mr. Dunn got out of the pickup and followed her uncertainly, taken aback by her abrupt departure and not sure whether he was supposed to come in for some iced tea or not. Flee was not embarrassed when he looked through the screen door and saw her crying.

"Whatsamatter?" he asked in genuine amazement. He would never have been able to imagine her crying if he hadn't seen it for himself.

"I don't really see why they had ta kill 'em," Flee answered him. Her voice was not wavering or weak.

"Those cats? You know we gotta kill cats."

"Babies?"

"They start gettin' big and they start gettin' calves. Might already have fer all we know. Cain't afford ta lose a buncha calves."

"They weren't killin' calves!" Flee's voice rose angrily. "They were just comin' in ta water. That ol' lion was just tryin' ta keep 'em alive and was barely stayin' alive herself." Mr. Dunn said nothing, but fingered the handle of the screen door, still not clear on the status of his invitation to tea. Flee's argument wasn't very practical, but he was wise enough not to try to talk sense to a crying woman. "You can tell by lookin' the mama wasn't killin' anything," my sister started again after a brief silence, "and there's a lot a' durn things that can kill a calf before those babies would ever have gotten around ta doin' it."

"Is Ernest here?" Mr. Dunn inquired politely, figuring the best thing he could do now was change the subject. "I needed ta see what kinda price he thought I oughta get fer ol' Rebel. I'm afraid he's just gonna go lame the minute I start tryin' ta use 'em hard again."

Flee scanned Mr. Dunn's face sharply, as though its bland features might have concealed some further understanding. Finding nothing there, she opened the screen door, and, with her body half outside the house and half in, pointed toward the corrals where Ernest was busy setting a new post. "He's over there," she said. She watched Mr. Dunn as he crossed the yard, and then, before she went back into the house, she turned her gaze toward the mountains, half-closing her eyes to shield them from the white sun.

8   Green Gate Cow

INSOFAR AS A RANCHING BUSINESS can be kept track of, my grandparents kept track of theirs in a large, leather-hinged ledger, recording, along with such items as the number of pounds of cake fed during the winter and the purchase of new pickup tires, the name of every cow and bull in their herd and the date of birth (and occasionally death) and sex of each new calf. Ranchers can, of course, tell one cow from another. The average person, under no constraints to learn to do so, cannot, and may even find it quite extraordinary that it matters in the least which cow was seen loitering at the Rock Tank last Wednesday, though clearly if there is a reason to doubt the health of that cow or to suspect she might have crawled into the neighbor's pasture, it matters immensely that she was alive and well . . . and around . . . on Wednesday. There are as many reasons for ranchers to know their cows as there are for scholars to know their books, reasons all implied in the generality that it is their business to know. In a casual survey, one cow may indeed look very much like another (as most humans do), but subtle differences in physique, color, personality, and habits, to which the rancher is attuned, render each animal unique to him, as the names in my grandparents' ledger may serve to illustrate.

In 1971, for example, my grandparents owned Wide Horns, Bushy Tail, Hazel Eye, Speckle Face, and Yellow Long Horn, as well as Meany, The Ugly Cow, The Fighting Cow, and Pet. Although the novice might have been hard-pressed to pick Bushy Tail out of the herd—chances are her tail was only a hair or two more bushy than Hazel Eye's and that Hazel Eye's eyes were hazel only when the sun hit them at certain angles—to my grandparents her distinguishing feature was quite vivid. The subtle gradations of (mostly bad) temper that differentiated Meany from Pet, much less Meany from The Fighting Cow, might not have been apparent to the inexperienced onlooker (had any of these ever ventured into the remote area where the ranch was situated), but my grandparents would have been familiar with the idiosyncrasies of each animal and would have known that, whereas Meany merely shoved other cows away from the water trough, The Fighting Cow was usually not satisfied until she had put them to flight.

The origins of many of the names in the ledger are not as self-explanatory as these, but we can speculate about them with some confidence. The cow called Crumple Horn West surely sported at least one crumpled horn and lived in the West Pasture. The biographies of Little Lecheguilla and Lecheguilla must have been quite similar—

each cow no doubt crippled herself on one of the sharp, stiff leaves of these cacti—even if their sizes were not. Fat Dawson was either purchased from my grandparents' neighbors, the Dawsons, or preferred grazing in their pastures and was always to be found in them. She might have been fat when she first came to the ranch, or she might have stayed fat even in "lean" years, or maybe she was never fat in her life, in which case the appellation was ironical. Or—is our conjecturing getting out of hand here?—Fat Dawson resembled some member of the Dawson family quaintly nicknamed "Fat" by the locals for his (or her) own capacity to maintain an ample girth in lean years.

Finally, the ledger contains names that cannot be glossed even by a person familiar with cows, with the customary ways in which they come by their names, or with my grandparents and their habits. Who, for example, were Little China, Little Marian, Unknown Number Two, Simona, and Georgie? My grandmother had a sister named Marian, but what the connection is, if indeed one exists, between the cow and my great aunt (a lovely, fastidious woman, who might not have been flattered to have a Hereford for a namesake, though she'd have been too polite to say so) remains a mystery. Thereby hangs a tale no doubt, but regrettably it perished with the passing of my grandparents, whose wonderful ledger, nevertheless, preserves the traditions of the family ranch in which every member of the "family" merited a name.

My father, too, knew all his cows down to the last horn and speckle (and the rest of us knew some of the more colorfully marked ones), but we never actually named them (there were too many) except when we were inspired to do so, as we were in the case of the Brahman cow my father bought at the Roswell Auction and hauled home in the covered stock trailer. "Got 'er dirt cheap," he told us proudly. Not dirt cheap enough, we all decided before the day was over.

My brother, sister, and I had gotten home from school and were starting the evening chores when my father drove up. We stopped what we were doing to help him unload and pen the contents of the trailer. My mother had come out of the house, still wearing her apron, and now stood by the waterlot fence, as curious as we were to see what my father had bought. About that time, a ferocious "Mmmmmmmmmmbaaarrrrr," delivered in a full bass voice, issued from the belly of the trailer. Peering through the slats, we could make out a grey shape, attached to the head of which were a pair of lengthy horns and two long, drooping ears. "Kinda cute little ol' bramer, isn't she?" my father joked out the pickup window as he positioned the trailer. "You shoulda seen 'em tryin' ta load 'er."

"Mmmmmmmmbaaaarrrr," muttered the cow, who apparently had enjoyed her ride even less than she had anticipated she might. As soon as the back end of the trailer was within the confines of the waterlot fence, my mother unfastened the tailgate to let out the unhappy creature, but before she could swing it all the way open, the cow made for the thin strip of sunlight suddenly admitted into her gloomy cell. My mother perceived that if she did not vacate her current location with all possible speed, she would be smashed by the gate, which was about to be knocked the rest of the way open by the fleeing cow. Therefore, with an athletic, adrenalin-inspired leap, (and to the accompaniment of my father shouting "Della! Della! Della!" unable, in his concern for her safety, to articulate more fully than that what it was he was shouting about), she got herself to a spot just beyond the arc that, a half-second later, the trailer gate whistlingly inscribed in the empty air.

The cow was "a little huffy" (as my father put it when relating this incident, a couple of days after it happened, to a friend) when she emerged from the trailer into the waterlot, but the fact that my mother now found herself standing a good six feet into that same enclosure would not ordinarily have augured any particular danger. Most animals in the condition known as "huffy" would have tried to get as far as possible as fast as possible from the source of their huffiness. After charging out of the trailer, they would have continued on through the waterlot and into the milk-cow pen, in whose nethermost corners they would have backed themselves, their horns aimed outward at the "enemy."

This cow, however, violated all the rules and sprang from the trailer in the posture of a fierce lion springing into an arena full of gladiators. She was ready to pounce on anything that moved, including my mother, whose image caught at her peripheral vision as a thorny bush catches at cloth. She twisted her body virtually in midflight and landed with the tips of her horns just touching the seat of my mother's britches. Perceiving as quickly as she had earlier that she was not in a very good place, my mother dashed for the trailer, the only haven available to her, with the cow hot on her trail. (My mother claimed later that, though she had suffered no bruises, the hip pocket had been ripped off her pants. How this happened none of us fully understood, for she ran, as one tends to in this situation, with her hands behind her back, palms turned outward to protect that tender part of her anatomy most at risk.)

Ordinarily, my mother's reactions would, again, have stood her in good stead, since normal cows do not voluntarily reenter the very confinement out of which they have just broken. The grey Brahman, however, had no compunction about jumping back into the trailer and every compunction about wasting an opportunity to get even with those who had dared trifle with her. Cows are territorial beasts, and, strangely enough, they do not like being uprooted from their accustomed haunts, whisked away in a contraption that rattles so much they can't think straight or get their bearings, and then dumped out in some "foreign country" where the water tastes funny. Tremors in their external environments can lead to major upheavals in their internal ones, in the throes of which they are unlikely to notice whether someone is trying to help or harm them. To the Brahman cow, my mother was "guilty" because she was human, a logic not entirely without merit; therefore, she chased her up into the trailer and might have skewered her there had not my mother had the presence of mind to slam the partition gate that divided the trailer in half. My mother was safe.

But she was also trapped in the nose of the trailer and likely to remain so as long as the cow rampaged in the rear of it, for we, the horrified spectators of this conflict, felt little inclination to interfere with a cow in as black a mood as this one was in. We had some presentiment of my mother's mood darkening to comparably somber hues if she were not released soon, but a mad Brahman can do great harm before coming to her senses, while my mother had never been known to inflict serious injury on any living creature, even in her worst moments. Therefore, common sense would surely have dictated that things remain as they were for quite some time if the cow had not decided, for obscure reasons, that she had punished my mother enough. Perhaps she was satisfied with the poetic justice of having imprisoned her victim in the very chamber she, herself, had been imprisoned in. Or perhaps, though she dreamed of baking my mother's children in a pie and serving them to her for supper, she recognized the impracticality of such a revenge. Whatever the case, she spun around immediately after the automatic latch of the partition clicked closed, sailed back out of the trailer, and ran to the center of the waterlot.

It was clear from the way she surveyed the fences, however, that she had no intention to remain for long in the waterlot, and, not surprisingly, she took her exit shortly thereafter and not in traditional fashion. She passed through a wooden gate, but it happened to be closed at the time. Next, she leaped effortlessly over a barbed wire gate, and finally, she disappeared into the thicketed draws of the Horse Pasture. My father, who had little opportunity to say or do anything (besides yell "Della, Della, Della"), so rapidly had these events transpired, "durned 'er ol' hide" when he beheld the splintery remains of his wooden gate. He then asked my mother if she were okay. "I'm gonna slit 'er throat if my cornbread's burned," was all my mother replied as she emerged from the trailer. We took that to mean that she had not been materially injured.

During supper that night, my sister observed admiringly that the grey Brahman had jumped like the horse in "National Velvet" and that she had headed *absolutely* due west from the moment she quit the center of the waterlot, "givin' ground ta nobody and no thing." My little brother, however, to be quarrelsome, pointed out that she would had to have gone slightly northwest to get from the wooden to the wire gate and that she had, in fact, swerved once, shying violently as she ran past still another gate, which hung between the waterlot and the milk-cow pen and which he had whiled away part of the summer after the first grade (when he was supposed to be cleaning out the saddle house) painting a bright green. As supper progressed and as we argued over the details of the story of my mother being loaded in the trailer by a cow, we began to call the Brahman who had done the deed the "Green Gate Cow," by which name she was known to us for the rest of her days.

A short time later, my father spotted his new acquisition in High Lonesome, the pasture furthest west and furthest removed from the house, and the one in which she elected to stay, usually by herself, also for the rest of her days. She chose as her *corencia,* or favorite spot, a wide draw, densely matted with mesquite and catclaw, that emptied into the Pecos River. Had she not found a place to her liking, she would in all probability have quitted the Heart-Diamond entirely and roamed the shores of the Pacific Ocean, for she respected neither fence nor gate. We attempted to move her, along with the rest of the cows, out of High Lonesome a few months later to "rest" the pasture. But not many days elapsed between the one on which we herded her across the ranch to the Lake Pasture and the one on which we glimpsed her grey back and high, shining horns gliding just above the surface of the brush in her draw. Several cowboys and a good part of a morning were "spent" in the effort to rout her again. So when she made her way back to High Lonesome a second and then a third time, leaving broken posts and dangling wires in the wake of her passage, my father decided that he wanted to keep her there after all and that we needn't bother her much except to wean or brand her calves.

However, bothering her even on these rare occasions produced effects not unlike prodding a rattlesnake with a stick. We invariably regretted it, in other words, and especially when we found ourselves rebuilding whatever pen we had been naive enough to suppose might hold her. The best we could ever hope for was that she'd jump the fence. Usually, however, if we got her to the pen at all, she'd search every inch of it until she found a loose wire. Then, inserting her long, narrow nose in the spaces resulting from the slack, she'd push until all the staples came out of the posts or until the posts came out of the ground. She preferred going through to jumping over. Once, she tore down the entire side of the pen by hurling her body into the net wire, freeing not only herself but her weaning-aged calf and half the rest of the "gather" too. Another time, she galloped through the gate with the other cattle, whirled around when she reached the back of the pen, and galloped back out the gate, so effectively intimidating, with a dramatic flourish of her horns, the hand who had dismounted to close it that he merely jumped aside and watched her go. Most times, however, we never got her anywhere near a set of pens. When her passions were roused, she had no qualms about charging horses, who did, on the other hand, have qualms about arguing with determined, horned cows, and who usually stepped aside, like the hand on the gate, to let her pass. Since her calves nearly always followed her in these daring getaways, many of them did not get branded until they were yearlings or sold until they were practically grown.

After one particularly trying encounter with the Green Gate Cow, during which she tore up the float on the water trough (she jumped into the trough to get past a hand who thought he had her cornered against it) and then injured a horse, my father threatened to take her back where she had come from, the Roswell Auction. When my mother playfully reminded him that he'd have to catch her and hold her first, he naturally vowed to do just that, though for several days he seemed at a loss as to how to carry out his vow and remained too deep in thought to engage in normal conversation. Strange smiles played upon his lips and weird glints lit up his eyes. At last he emerged from this state and ordered my little brother to paint all the gates in the Big Pen, the stoutest and highest of the house pens, a bright green. We wondered, naturally, if he were not suffering from some form of mild insanity. "That'll take me a week," protested my brother, a notorious dawdler. "I expect ya can do it by tomorrow," my father growled, and my brother decided that, indeed, he probably could.

If he had wanted to, my father could have brought in the Green Gate Cow the day before the sale and either snubbed her to a post or left her loaded in the trailer all night (once he had figured out how to put her in it—he probably would have rejected the idea of using my mother for bait). Many ranchers would, in fact, have resorted to one of these repressive and unimaginative expedients in dealing with an animal as reprobate as she. The rancher who had managed to get her to the auction ring in the first place and the men working at the ring who had managed to get her into my father's trailer had not, in all probability, handled her with kid gloves. But the truth was, in spite of the damage she had inflicted on the various facilities and inhabitants of the Heart-Diamond (or really because of it), she had earned a certain amount of respect. Just as a soldier might honor a valiant foe by sparing his life, so my father, out of grudging admiration for the Green Gate Cow's stubborn refusal to be domesticated, wished to spare her such brutal treatment, although it was surely the only kind that would ever prevail against her own unscrupulous tactics.

Furthermore, she now had a reputation as a "critter with some life in 'er,'" which she conferred upon the rest of the ranch even though most of the other critters who lived on the Heart-Diamond were comparatively dull. According to my father's philosophy at least, she deserved the fighting chance that sheer force, however much she resisted it, would effectively deprive her of. Besides, my father always preferred outwitting to overpowering his animals. And it may have been the case, too, that he did not, deep down, *really* want to get rid of the Green Gate Cow.

My father had never spelled out these notions for us, of course, but we had pieced them together over time. Still, even in the context of such principles, the plan to paint all the Big Pen gates green in hopes that the cow wouldn't jump over or through them seemed a little farfetched. But we were careful how we teased him about it. In the first place, he "knew" cattle better than we did, and we were reluctant to crawl too far out on a limb that might well break beneath us. In the second, we sensed that *he* was feeling a little sheepish about the idea, now that he had aired it in public, and that he, too, knew it had been hatched by that minute fraction of his brain that was not, as the rest of his brain was, eminently stable, rational, and incapable of the outlandish and the bizarre. Finally, in consequence of his embarrassment no doubt, he did not like to be teased about it. My mother ventured once to call it a "farmer plan," because she said, it reminded her of our farmer friend who built the duck blind by the gate so he could shut up his old wild cow when she came in for water. (Most of the farmers in the area owned a few head of cattle, which they never quite knew how to manage.) My father was not amused.

But if he were embarrassed by it, he still persisted in it, for he was more curious than embarrassed. He had surely conceived the idea while repairing the aftermath of one of the cow's "romps" through the fences, and, although initially he had recognized it as a fantasy—as a self-gratifying daydream about mastering the renegade cow—it had gradually begun to intrigue him. Most likely, my little brother had not seen the cow shy at all, or if he had, he'd seen her shy at a rabbit or a cat running through the pen, not at the green gate. In other words, there was no very substantial evidence that, confronted by a green gate, the Green Gate Cow would not do to it what she did to other gates. But whether she would or not would never be known unless it were put to the test, and someday we might need to know. My father's plan had evolved into a scientific experiment, which, though the knowledge it yielded might have no immediate practical application, could solve some vital problem in the future. Perhaps he would sell the cow, but mostly he wanted to find out if she were afraid of anything.

My father's crazy plan nearly succeeded, and it must be said in its behalf that the flaw was in the execution, not in the theory. We spent a day chasing the cow and her skittish calf out of the draw and driving them home. Once we had them in the Big Pen, they stayed there, the cow apparently stymied by the soundness of the fences and especially by the gaudy green gates, none of which she ever ventured near. "The gates needed painting," my mother said, "but I wouldn't go close to that color either." After a furious hour of snuffing and testing the sections of fence most removed from the gates, the cow seemed, for the first time since we had owned her, to accept her fate. Her calf was puzzled by the strange transformation in her behavior and sniffed questioningly at her as though he were checking for signs of injury or sickness.

My father perceptibly softened toward the cow when he saw that she had a phobia, maybe because he had his own phobia about birds. He spoke quietly, reassuring her that we weren't going to hurt her. Previously, the significance of her name had seemed to reside only in a brief and trivial incident, but now it deepened, and we realized that we had accidentally touched upon some deep dark secret of the cow's past the day we had begun calling her the Green Gate Cow. If any other rancher had bought her at the sale, her "weakness" would never have been exposed. Only my father's peculiarities had brought hers to light. "Somebody musta hit 'er between th' ears with a green post or somethin'," speculated my little brother about the origin of the cow's fear. He recalled a cow he'd heard about from a kid at school who lived on a ranch. This one had been so scared of trees that the kid's daddy had finally had to sell her to an "ol' boy" in West Texas. "Guess she was in a real state all right if she lived around here," my sister commented wryly. "Must be at least ten trees in Eddy County alone."

We were perched on the top rail of the Big Pen listening to Trey and watching the Green Gate Cow chew her cud. The sun was setting and the first traces of pink were showing through the edges of a couple of streaky clouds in an otherwise endless sky. "Reckin what kinda price she'd bring?" my father finally got around to asking my mother. She said she didn't know but pointed out that the cow "sure was in good shape and fixin' to have another calf." She had more or less forgiven the grey Brahman for chasing her into the trailer and was impressed by her size. My father agreed that the Green Gate Cow was, indeed, a prize specimen.

"Sure got an awful good calf on 'er now," he added. "Must weigh 375. An' she's not old."

At this juncture, my mother glanced at my father, trying to make out his face in the light of the fading sun, for at times its expressions would betray the direction his thoughts were tending. His lips were in a straight line. Since his lips were an external gauge upon which could be followed the tippings and tiltings of the mental balance he used to weigh arguments, she deduced that he had reached an impasse in the debate about whether or not to get rid of the cow and was now asking for outside mediation. She could understand his indecision. All the good reasons to sell the Green Gate Cow were equally good reasons to keep her.

"Of course those are all pretty good reasons to keep her too I guess," my mother volunteered, "and maybe she's gotten through her ornery stage. She seems awfully gentle now." Sure enough, the grey Brahman was behaving like an old milk cow. She flapped an enormous ear at a fly now and then, but was otherwise perfectly still and appeared to be dozing off, although her calf still eyed us warily.

"Oh, ya cain't ever tell," answered my father distractedly, unhelpfully vague as to which of my mother's observations you couldn't ever tell about. In decisions of this sort—the sort she figured she felt less strongly about than my father—she generally tried to help him justify to himself whatever course she thought his feelings were resolving him to follow. "Well . . ." she hesitated, hoping for some further clue.

As it turned out, my father did not get to decide whether he'd keep the Green Gate Cow or sell her. She seemed so civilized that when he entered the Big Pen to get a better look at her, he didn't bother to close the gate behind him. Perhaps he figured that if she made any move toward it, he'd just head her off, given how gentle she was now. Even after he had edged a good ways into the pen, she showed more interest in a few wisps of alfalfa hay that had blown up against the fence than in him. She casually dropped her nose to the ground and just as casually strolled over to the hay, followed by her wide-eyed calf. The position she took up by the fence, however, changed the configuration of the triangle whose three points were her, my father, and the gate, lengthening the leg between my father and shortening the one between her and the gate, so that when she broke for the opening, my father was too far away to interpose his body between her and it . . . which was probably just as well. He did manage to cut off the calf's escape, however, by shouting and waving his hat in its face. Thus was weaned the Green Gate Cow's calf this particular year, nor were any of the others ever separated from her with greater ease. "Why you ol' outfit," my father called as her figure retreated (where else?) into the setting sun.

We grew to appreciate, for more traditional reasons than her reputation for liveliness, the Green Gate Cow and to recognize that she was worth the trouble she caused. Her bull calves were invariably big and "framey," and when we did contrive to get them sold, they consistently outweighed any other yearling on the ranch. Her heifers, some of whom we kept, grew into productive cows, not one of whom exhibited any symptoms of her mother's temperament. One terribly droughty year, during which we were forced to supplement their normal diet of grass and weeds with cake and hay, many of the cows failed to conceive and most of them grew poor, but the Green Gate Cow stayed relatively fat and in the spring gave birth to another healthy half-Brahman baby, who also grew fat and sleek. She was the kind of cow who did well regardless of range conditions—a "doin" kind of cow who upheld the conviction of many ranchers that Brahmans were a little smarter and more resourceful than other breeds.

Furthermore, her escape from the Big Pen seemed to initiate a change in the mode of her opposition to us, perhaps because she learned from it that she could have her way with less physical effort than was requisite for destroying gates and pens. She no longer flung herself through fences unless all other strategies failed. The hunted look went out of her eye, giving way to a confident, crafty gleam. She began to wait for opportunities to get away rather than creating them, quickly taking advantage of any hand who had "gone to sleep" on the job. And, somewhat perversely, my father began to side with her and to "forget" to warn the hired hands to pay particular attention to "that ol' bramer cow in the corner," especially if one of them seemed overly proud of the talents of his cowhorse. "Yeah, I bought this ol' horse a couple a' months ago," one of these fresh-faced young heroes would invariably brag. "Nothin' gets past 'em."

"We'll see," my father would say to himself, grinning all the while. Age and experience had taught him that, as the saying goes, "there ain't a hoss that cain't be rode, and there ain't a cowboy that cain't be throwed." He also knew, however, how futile it was to try to impart such wisdom to young cowhands. He let the Green Gate Cow do it instead, chuckling appreciatively as she invariably slid by the touted horse, although he always handled tactfully the hand's wounded pride. As the cow's escapes grew more subtle and less spectacular, the cowboys whose admiration she had once excited grew less interested in her, even though she continued to outmaneuver them. But my father considered her a more formidable and imaginative adversary than ever. "Why you ornery ol' cuss," he'd murmur fondly as she disappeared, once again, over a distant hill.

One day, when he was riding through High Lonesome to check on things, he decided to hunt up the Green Gate Cow, mostly just to keep her on her toes . . . and himself on his. He struck some tracks disappearing into the brush of the big draw, and, figuring that they could possibly be hers, followed them for a mile or so, finally catching sight of her as she pushed her way through some mesquite. He got enough of a look to tell that she'd probably just had another calf, and he decided he'd have a look at the calf, too . . . just to see if he could find it.

It is a cow's instinct, as it is some birds' and other animals', to protect her newborn calf by luring intruders away from its hiding place. The mother cow will pretend to be searching for her calf or going to it, when actually she is moving further and further away from it. As she walks along, she may pause occasionally to stare about, as though trying to remember in which bush or clump of grass it was she instructed her young one to lie while she made the long trip to water. The experienced cowhand doesn't fall for this "I think I left him right here" ploy, of course, and counters it with a ploy of his own. He knows that if the mother grows truly anxious, she'll make a beeline for the baby or at least betray its hiding place with an uneasy glance. The strategy, therefore, is to worry her a bit, and this is accomplished by imitating, as closely as possible, the cry of a small calf in trouble. Partially muffling his mouth with his hand to soften his voice and to create a tremolo effect, the cowboy utters something like "mmmmbeh reh reh reh reh" or "mmmmmbeeeehhhhh" or whatever it is he thinks a calf says when it needs its mama's help. He repeats the cry until the cow cannot resist assuring herself that her little one is safe.

"Beh reh reh reh reh," my father called, trying to get the Green Gate Cow's attention. She did not look back or slow down but kept up a steady pace through the brush. He followed her by listening for the snap of breaking twigs and branches. "Mmmmbeh reh reh reh reh," he cried more loudly and urgently, but the Green Gate Cow continued to plow through the draw. In fact, she increased her speed a fraction, for which reason my father decided that she had divined his mission and was not about to fall for the "beh reh reh reh reh" trick. She had probably stashed the calf at the other end of the draw and had no intention of going anywhere near it now.

He was making up his mind to abandon his search—after all, he didn't really need to see the calf—when he burst through a particularly dense stand of mesquite brush into a grassy low place, in the center of which stood a large dark bush and the Green Gate Cow. The cow was staring intently at the bush when my father appeared, but then she turned to look at him (nervously he thought) for a second or two before walking away (or tearing herself away, he thought) from the bush. When she reached the edge of the clearing, she glanced at him challengingly and at the bush furtively.

"Ah hah!" exclaimed my father and rode over to inspect the environs of the bush. Although one of the branches cradled a sloppily constructed buzzards' nest, none of the shadowy dens at its base concealed a baby calf. But my father knew that the calf could be lying virtually at his horse's feet and not be visible because of its coloring and immobility. And in fact, the Green Gate Cow now appeared to be quite anxious. Lifting her nose high, she sniffed the air, sizing up her pursuer through the scent she caught of him. Then, seemingly in spite of a monumental effort not to take any particular notice of the spot through which my father's large horse now blundered and plodded, she emitted the guttural whisper, unique to Brahman cows, in which they talk to their young. "Ah hah!" chortled my father again. "Beh reh reh reh reh." This time he bawled in a sobbing, broken voice calculated to tear the heartstrings of any caring parent to shreds. "Mmmmmbawwwww," replied the Green Gate Cow angrily, as though she suspected the intruder of harming her baby. She swung around to face my father like a battle tank, her head held erect to show off her menacing horns to best advantage. She pawed the ground a time or two and took a step toward the horse, the light breeze snatching at the dirt she stirred up. Two hawks circling miles above watched the scene lazily. My father sat very still. The phenomenon of a cow defending her helpless calf, even though she, herself, might be subjected to danger in doing so, always interested and moved him.

"I won't hurt yer baby, ol' girl," he told her, and then he left, not wanting to agitate her anymore.

As he backtracked down the draw, my father was thinking to himself how odd it was that a cow as shrewd as the Green Gate Cow had been so easy to deceive. His imitation of a calf in distress had sent her scrambling toward her baby, although she had pulled herself sufficiently together at the last minute to go into her "act." But even then, a few more "beh reh rehs" would have made her go to the calf (although probably only after she had charged the horse). It all went to show that you "cain't ever tell."

About this time, a froliscome little breeze, in a burst of energy, lifted my father's Stetson off his head and deposited it on a nearby patch of grama grass. My father was glad that nobody saw him lose his hat. Cowboys aren't supposed to lose their hats even in tornadoes, a "rule" formulated by that grim-faced master, experience—horses don't like for Stetsons to sail past their eyes unexpectedly—but one that had gradually assumed the unrelenting visage of a social *faux pas*. He got off his horse to retrieve the hat, which of course bounded away just as he touched it and might have proved a tiresomely provoking truant had it not gotten itself stuck in the thorny branches of a catclaw, where it hung dejectedly, waiting to be picked up and put back to work.

As my father led his horse toward the bush (glad that there were no witnesses to the spectacle of his chasing the hat either), he happened to glimpse a shiny white object lying in the grass about five feet away. Under close scrutiny, the white object resolved itself into a snowy marking on the forehead of a tiny grey heifer calf. "Ah hah," said my father, but this time his tone was different. The Green

Gate Cow had tricked him after all. The calf was curled in a ball in a particularly tall clump of grass (my father's earlier tracks passed within a foot of her nose) with her neck stretched flat along the ground. She had obviously been instructed by her mother to lie low, and was doing precisely that. But she was too new to the world to be truly frightened and did nothing except close her huge eyes and twitch her long Brahman ears when my father scratched her head, as though she enjoyed the sensation. Her hair had been licked immaculately clean into silky swirls and "cowlicks." My father enjoyed the beauty of the calf's vulnerable innocence for a moment more. Then he clapped his hat on his head and pulled it a good half inch below the tan line on his forehead.

A month or so later during the spring roundup, my father assigned himself the task of "gathering" the Green Gate Cow and her heifer calf, assuming that, in spite of the outcome of their earlier "contest," he'd probably come nearer accomplishing that task than anybody else. The calf would have grown considerably by now and would be less difficult to find. Starting at the watering place on the river nearest the cow's *corencia*, he followed the trail she probably usually used to return to the draw after she had drunk. After not too long a search, he found her standing in a clearing similar to the one in which she had staged her "mother cow" routine for him. Surprisingly, she did not crash away into the brush as she usually did when a cowboy appeared on the scene, and, in fact, my father realized before too long that she was behaving strangely. When he rode across the clearing toward her, she sidled away to his left, bawling loudly all the while. He noticed that her bag was swollen with milk and that she had not been to water recently. Her flanks caved sharply inward, accentuating her already prominent hip bones. Apparently, something had happened to the heifer calf, though if the mother were still crying for it, she should also still be hanging around the carcass. There was no carcass in sight and no buzzards circling overhead. My father tried to start the Green Gate Cow out of the clearing, mainly just to see what she'd do, hoping that whatever she did would provide some clue to help him solve the mystery of her behavior. She refused to drive, entering the brush far enough to circle behind him and reenter the clearing. Afterwards, she was too distressed to pay much attention to him at all and stood and bawled mournfully at a prickly pear, around which she had walked so many times she had worn a trail in the hard ground.

At first, my father thought the Green Gate Cow was "alkalied"—that is, that she had eaten grass growing in the alkaline soil near the river. At certain times of the year or after particular weather patterns, the grass draws the poisonous mineral up into its shoots. Alkalied cattle generally stop eating and drinking, grow blind and disoriented, and walk in tight circles before dying. But the Green Gate Cow was not staggering, nor did she appear to be fevered or blind. The circle she was walking seemed purposeful, not random. My father scanned the clearing again for signs of the calf, but from where he sat he could see nothing. He backed his horse into the edge of the brush to watch the cow. Immediately, she stopped walking and mooed at the prickly pear. My father was baffled and had begun to think that the cow was mentally deranged, alkali or no alkali, and that she probably didn't remember she even had a calf, when suddenly the probable cause for her strange actions dawned on him.

Quickly spurring his horse toward the prickly pear,

my father discovered the mouth of a shallow sinkhole that the pear and a stubble of salt grass had heretofore concealed from him. This section of the Heart-Diamond was dotted with such holes; new ones opened up after rains softened the ground. Some old ranchers contended that all of southeastern New Mexico sat on ground as hollow as the Carlsbad Caverns and that sinkholes were just a preview of what would someday happen to "the whole durn region" (greatly to the detriment of the ranching industry, needless to say). As my father moved in to get a better view of this one (which had, in fact, swallowed up part of his herd, albeit a small part), the Green Gate Cow snorted loudly but did not back away, and when he dismounted to peer into it, she peered too, breathing literally down his collar.

The initial shaft of the hole was wide enough, although not deep enough, to engulf a Shetland pony. There was a smaller deeper hole within the first one, which angled off in a northerly direction, but my father could not tell exactly how deep it was because the mouth, nose, and eyes of the lost heifer calf were blocking the entrance. "Mmmaaaarrrr," she called pitifully when she heard the activity around her, to which the Green Gate Cow responded with a series of grunts followed by a piercing shriek. "Fer Pete's sake," my father scolded, swiveling around in his squatting position to find the cow's face in his. "Would ya get outta my ear before ya do that again?"

"Baaarrrrrrrr," answered the cow at even more stentorian decibels. Her brown eyes, into whose liquid depths my father now gazed, were rounded with fear and anxiety. She had jumped a startled step backwards when he moved and spoke to her, but now craned her neck, her nose hovering at his cheek and touching it occasionally, the way a bee bounces on a flower. It occurred to my father that if she decided he was a threat to her calf, she would run over him right here and now. But even though she bobbed her head up and down and shuffled her feet, as cows sometimes do when they are angry, she did not seem hostile, only upset. "You better let me help ya a little," my father said to her in mild tones he hoped she'd find soothing to her frayed nerves. He could feel a wet spot on his cheek as, still squatting, he pivoted on the soles of his feet to face the hole again, being careful not to make the move a sudden one.

The heifer calf was thoroughly stuck. The edges of the larger hole had probably collapsed beneath her weight as she passed near it, and she had slipped, hind feet first, into the narrower shaft. As she had scrabbled around with her front feet trying to pull herself out, more ground had given way and her struggles had served only to wedge her more tightly into the opening. At least this is all my father could imagine had happened. He had found lots of animals in sinkholes but none in quite the predicament this one was in. She looked miserable and gazed forlornly at him.

"What're ya doin' in there?" my father asked for lack of anything better to say. Again, it was his hope that a gentle voice would ease the distress of both mother and child. He already could not get his hand past the point of the heifer's shoulder. If she were frightened into struggling again, she might slip even farther into the shaft, in consequence of which her rescue would pose certain engineering problems my father was not certain he could solve. Even now, only one method of extracting her was possible, and my father, straightening up slowly and proceeding cautiously to his horse, made preparations to implement it, all the while keeping a careful eye on the cow, who kept a careful eye on him. He unfastened his rope from his saddle, and, as he carried it back to the sinkhole, formed in it a loop large enough to fit over the calf's head. Since he could not slip the rope any farther down her body than her neck, she'd have to be pulled out at the risk of being choked to death.

Having placed the loop around the heifer's neck, my father remounted his horse and dallied the other end of the rope twice around his saddle horn, backing the horse until the slack in the rope disappeared. When the calf did not budge, he turned the horse's head away from the hole, and the stout creature, feeling the pressure of the rope and comprehending what was expected of him, dropped his shoulders and pulled mightily. For an eternal moment, nothing gave, and my father could hear the raw gasps of the strangling calf. He knew she couldn't take much more, and so, in an all-or-nothing gamble, he touched his spurs to the horse, who shot forward when the calf popped out of the hole and dragged the body two or three yards before my father could pull him up. Dismounting and running quickly to the little heifer, my father removed the rope and massaged her windpipe. She lay jerking and twitching, fighting to suck the air back into her depleted lungs. At last, though she made no offer as yet to get up, she began to breathe more easily, and my father knew she would be fine as soon as she collected her wits and rested a little. He decided to leave her alone so that her mother, who had been startled by the horse's lunge and was now standing a good ten yards away, would come to her and lap her with her rough tongue.

Catching up his trailing reins, he was about to raise his

left foot to the stirrup when he remembered he had tightened his cinch earlier to prevent the saddle from being pulled to one side during the rescue and that it needed to be let out a notch or two. He led the horse out of the way so that he could perform this operation without delaying the reunion of the mother and her baby. The instant the path was cleared, the cow was at the heifer's side, exploring the small body with her nose. Shortly afterwards, the heifer heaved herself onto her feet, reached greedily for a swollen udder, and closed her eyes blissfully as the first swallow of warm milk passed down her throat.

Leaning against his horse, over whose muscular neck he had draped one arm, my father watched the cow and calf. The Green Gate Cow bent her head around to smell the calf again, as if to confirm, once and for all, that it had been restored to her unharmed. Then she gave vent to a trumpety "maaaawwwwww," which my father took the liberty of interpreting as a "thank you very much."

"Don't mention it," he replied politely. He felt good about the happy ending he had brought about. He turned toward his horse and began to pull the latigo through the D-ring. The Green Gate Cow was no longer in his line of vision, but he continued to converse with her as he fiddled with the cinch. "You've gotten awful careless in yer ol' age," he chided her. "You better watch that baby better. I might not show up next time." The sky was a fathomless azure, and heat waves floated just above the surface of the grassy flat that came up to the edge of the draw. It seemed to my father, as he looked around at the Heart-Diamond stretching before him in every direction, that for once, everything was in place, and that he could almost hear the deep slow hum of . . . something, of the earth perhaps or of nature, although the actual sound that broke the afternoon stillness was the sound of breaths being drawn and expelled—the calf's (she had stopped nursing), the cow's, the horse's, his own.

He put the tongue of the buckle through the appropriate hole in the latigo and ran the trailing end of the leather strap back through the top D-ring to keep it out of the way. He became more conscious of the fact that the Green Gate Cow, rather than trotting off to hide in the brush, had chosen to remain in the clearing and was now grazing peacefully. He could hear her pulling up the grass. He glanced over his shoulder at her and found her considering him nonchalantly, grinding up grass as she did so with a slow, circular motion of her jaws. Her eyes, in fact, were vacant and half-closed, and she seemed the perfect image of contentment—a contented cow if there ever was one—as did her calf, who stood with her forehead against her mother's flank. "We've been through the wringer together, haven't we ol' girl?" my father addressed the cow, oddly gratified that she had not run away from him. "These silly kids." She stopped chewing long enough to bat an ear at a fly and then resumed chewing.

My father prepared to mount his horse. He placed his left foot in the stirrup once more, grasping his reins and the saddle horn with his left hand. His right hand brushed the saddle skirts, which had once been a shiny burnt orange and so stiff they had chaffed his thighs. They had gradually softened, through the operations of sweat and usage, to a deep tan, much the color of the skin on the hand that touched them now. My father grabbed the cantle with his right hand, poised to pull himself up onto the horse, thinking, now that the excitement was over and his energies had subsided to normal levels, that getting on a horse wasn't as easy as it once had been—that what he had used to do in one smooth, automatic motion now required a summoning of effort and strength. "Reckin we're not silly kids anymore," he said aloud, more to himself than to the cow.

No sooner had these solemnly reflective words passed his lips than a jarring blow to the back of his knee crumpled his right leg, which had just been preparing to swing over the horse's back. If he had not been clutching the saddle, he would have collapsed to the ground. Astonished, he looked over his shoulder again and this time encountered the brazen stare of the calf, who had apparently already forgotten not only her recent plight but the identity of her savior.

"What in creation d'ya think *yer* doin', ya ornery little sow?" he inquired of the heifer, still not believing what had happened. Calves this young do not charge people, especially out in the middle of the pasture. "Yer not s'posed ta do that," my father informed the heifer. The blow, which she had delivered with her as yet hornless brow, had stunned her slightly and rocked her back on her heels, but she was gathering herself for another charge. My father sought the safety of his perch atop his tall horse, to whose knees the heifer did not quite reach. The Green Gate Cow bawled, trying to recall her calf, whose abrupt departure from her side and current proximity to the horse occasioned new fears and anxieties. "Yer gonna have yer hands full," my father said to the grey Brahman, whose answering "mmrrrr" clearly meant "what about you?" As he rode out of sight, my father saw the Green Gate Cow's Sinkhole Heifer trot unconcernedly back to her worried mama, of whom, except for the little patch of white on her forehead, she was the spitting image.

9 *Going Home*

"MILLER, YOU REMEMBER MY DAUGHTER Kathy, don'cha? Kathy, this is Miller Ammons. He used ta help put on th' Artesia kids' rodeo when you were still a kid." My father extended his left arm toward me to draw me into the conversation he was having with an ancient man wearing a black felt hat. The hair not covered by the hat was thick and paper white; the cheeks, bunched into puffy pouches by too many years of proximity to a grinning mouth, were red over a dark western tan, as though they had recently been exposed to a cold wind; and the eyes, from the corners of which deep lines trailed off toward the temples, were glowing and vigorous. Everybody I'd ever heard mention Mr. Ammons said he was pretty feisty to be ninety, and the energy his dark eyes radiated confirmed those observations. With his marvelously bowed legs and his Levis tucked into the fancy tops of high-heeled, hand-tooled boots, he resembled a piece of western sculpture.

As I reached to shake hands with him, I momentarily forgot I was in a bad humor and thought of my fried Pat, a folklorist at the midwestern university where I attended graduate school, and from which I was, at the moment, on a short break. Pat would love to add this man to his collection of what he admiringly called "vestiges," elderly people who had worked at jobs and professions requiring kinds of "know-how" that modern technologies had made obsolete. Because they no longer initiated succeeding generations into the arts of their various callings, these were being lost, so Pat recorded the life histories of his vestiges, their accounts and descriptions of the talents nobody paid them to exercise anymore, and their notions about the "improvements" that had supplanted them.

Although machines have yet to replace the horse, the rope, and the person capable of managing them both at the same time, the advent of cattle trucks, feedlots, squeeze chutes, and computers have changed the shape of ranching enough to obviate certain skills connected, for example, with the long cattle drive or with branding outside the confines of a holding pen. Miller was a real "ol' timey" cowboy, my father had said once. "He's forgotten more than I ever learned." I felt the same way about my father—that he knew things he wasn't teaching my brother, sister, and me because we had no use for them— and sometimes fretted that cowboy culture would disappear altogether. "Pat should meet this man," I said to myself, "and he probably oughtta do it pretty soon." To Mr. Ammons I merely said "how ya doin'?" in the drawl that had once been my "native" tongue, but which I now had to practice two or three days each time I came home for a visit before it was natural for me again.

Going away from home had been good for me, or at least I thought so most of the time. Now when I returned, I did so with a new appreciation of the Southwest—of its immensity and its peace—and with the good sense to regard my childhood as having been special, even privileged. On the other hand, I never was, and never wanted to be, entirely out of touch. After particularly trying periods in graduate school, when I felt burned out, fed up, and done in, I always headed home to soak myself in the currents of life that flowed through the Heart-Diamond. This particular break had fallen in the aftermath of one of those enervating periods. I had just completed my general exams, and my batteries needed recharging. "I gotta go to New Mexico," I had informed my roommate, who stayed away from her parents as much as possible.

There had been times, probably during my second year of graduate school after the excitement had died down a little, when I had worried about how much I missed home and my family. I imagined myself still talking about "daddy" when I was eighty years old, frozen in my past, my brain a museum of Pollyannish memories of the good old days of my youth. My roommate once claimed she felt lucky to have a poor relationship with her folks because not cutting loose from home kept you from reaching your full potential as an individual. "Boy, you really *do* get along with your parents," she had accused me after overhearing one of my phone conversations with them. "Cain't help it," I had apologized.

I tried to explain to her about going home. "Something happens to me over St. Louis," I said, at which juncture she looked skeptical. She was from Albany and didn't believe anything significant could ever happen to anybody *in* St. Louis, much less over it. "That's where the plane turns southwest and heads for Dallas," I persisted, ignoring her look. "The Dallas airport is where I see the first western hats and where I begin to feel I'm home. Before the plane gets to St. Louis, I'll be rewriting a seminar paper in my head or wondering what Professor Johnson really meant when she said 'hi' to me in the hall. Then the pilot tilts the wing down over the golden arch to make the turn to Dallas, and that's when I start thinking about my parents waiting for me in El Paso. They pick me up, and we drive to Carlsbad. By the time we get there, we've caught up on each other's news."

"Going to the country and getting away from it all," my roommate had summarized.

"Not exactly that. Going home isn't getting away from anything. It's getting into something different. When I'm trying to pry open the jaws of a sick cow and poke some feed down her throat, I don't care anymore what Professor Johnson meant. I figure she meant what she said, and if she didn't, she oughtta just say so. What matters really is whether or not the cow starves to death. What matters really is that Shakespeare knew there were people who cared more about their hungry turkeys and the sore spots on their horses' backs than about the wars their 'superiors' were plotting. He liked those people. You see what I mean?"

"Ooh, a sick cow!"

Mr. Ammons' dry hand gripped mine, which was soft now and free of all callouses except for a large one my pen had rubbed on my middle finger. "Why shore I remember Kathy," he replied to my father with genuine enthusiasm.

"How ya doin' young lady? Where's them pigtails ya useta wear?"

"Well, I reckin I'm not that young anymore." I smiled at him, pleased by his hearty greeting.

"Hell, y'ain't old." He still held my hand and shook it several more times before releasing it. "Now when ya get ta be as old as I am, then yer old. Hell, you can still climb on a horse, cain't cha? I cain't do that no more." As he spoke, he walked toward my black mare, Lucera, whom I had been saddling when my father had beckoned to me. He adjusted the girth so it wouldn't be twisted when I pulled it under the mare's belly to fasten it. "Course that excuse gets me outta doin' a lotta work I'd otherwise haveta do. Leaves me time ta rip around in that ol' pickup an' visit a little. I come out here ta th' arena ta watch these young fellers rope steers an' tell 'em how ta do it. Keeps me in touch, an' course they jus' 'preciate th' hell outta it."

"Well, I guess I can still climb on one," I acknowledged, keeping up the bantering tone. "But this ol' thing a' mine's hardly worth th' effort." I scratched the black mare, of whom I was inordinately fond, on the stomach, and she flapped her bottom lip appreciatively.

"Zat that ol' mare ya bought from Buck awhile back?" He addressed this question to my father, concealing behind a smile his shrewd appraisal of the mare's conformation. "Awhile back" had been at least ten years ago, but I was not surprised he recognized and remembered all about Lucera, even though he probably hadn't seen her more than once or twice before.

"Yeah, that's her," my father said. "She made a pretty good ol' mare. Stupid thing was scared ta death a' cattle when we got 'er. She'd been raised in a pen an' hadn't ever hearda' cows, I guess."

"Yeah, them's the kind donno how ta travel over anything 'cept smooth ground. They fall in holes an' stumble over rocks if ya don' watch'em ever' second. Wears ya out ta ride 'em."

"Yeah, we had ta put some time in on 'er, but ya know the silly ol' thing's a pretty good cowhorse now. Pretty good ropin' horse too."

"Well, my daddy always said there wasn't nothin' more persuasive with horses than time 'n patience. These young fellers today rig 'em up with all kindsa gadgets. Try ta make up fer the fact they donno nothin' 'bout trainin' one. Well, young lady," Mr. Ammons said, turning to me again, "I'll watch ya to see if ya can still throw a rope. Been practicin'?" He patted Lucera on the neck a last time and stepped back from her.

"Aw, not much." I had finished saddling up by this time. We had come to Artesia so my father and I could enter the "mixed" team roping together. The mixed roping is a special rodeo event in which one member of the two-person roping team must be an experienced or expert roper and the other a novice or a woman, the thinking being that a woman handicaps an expert to the same degree a novice does. Naturally, I resented such assumptions. However, I knew little about competitive steer roping, since it had become a popular sport only after I had gone to college. I was grateful nobody expected me to be any better than a beginner. Besides, my sister and several other women were in the process of reshaping these attitudes by winning many of the contests. No novice stood much chance against a good roper, man or woman.

"Well, ya can prob'ly outrope ol' Hart here even if ya ain't been practicin'," the old man teased, placing a hand on my father's shoulder.

"Won't take much ta do that," my father agreed.

I liked these kinds of conversations—felt at home with the lighthearted indirection of southwestern (and primarily "cowboy") speech. You had to listen for the meaning in the seemingly simple exchanges, whose casual understatements made the expression of serious emotions and ideas unembarrassing and therefore possible. Admittedly, having to "interpret" all the time occasionally resulted in unnecessarily hurt feelings. On the whole, however, I preferred the richly textured subtlety, with its inherent liability of being misunderstood, to barren forthrightness, with its inherent liability of being understood all too well.

It was through such subterranean and circuitous channels that my parents had gradually made me understand that they were proud of me for being in graduate school but not particularly interested in every twist and twitch of my career there. Certain silences and pauses, a manner of changing the topic of conversation, an unenthusiastic "izzatright?" at a critical point in a story I was telling—these clues communicated to me that graduate school was an experience I could not fully share with them, an important part of myself that could not be entirely integrated into my visits home.

And there were other small ways in which I was conscious of not quite fitting anymore. I was no longer completely sure of myself and hesitated sometimes before climbing down into a penful of milling cattle, flanking a calf, or mounting a skittish horse. I'd get annoyed when my brother or sister, to whom everything still came as naturally as breathing, helped me with some tool I'd half forgotten the use of. But I knew how clumsily I handled it.

These inadequacies had seemed particularly glaring to me for the last couple of days. I needed to be home more than ever but couldn't quite get there. I wanted my parents to know how worn out I was from studying, but they had teased me about sleeping late the first two mornings after my plane flight. The third day, my father, as though nothing important had happened in my life, had suggested we head for Artesia to rope steers. When we had gotten there, I had unloaded Lucera from the trailer and begun to saddle her with the same meaningful lack of appetite that had informed my mother's consumption of the, to my mind, juicy tidbits of gossip about my exams. "You wouldn't *believe* what my Eighteenth Century professor said when he handed me the questions! I could have died!" I had offered her this tantalizing morsel from my other world during the trip from El Paso. "Izzatright?" she had answered absently. "Hart, isn't that the Mexican restaurant we ate in when we came down for the wedding?" If my parents couldn't generate a spark or two for me, I certainly wasn't going to light up for them.

But Mr. Ammons' apparent interest made me feel better. He next wanted to know what I'd been "up to," and when I explained I was still going to school, he only caught the last word. "Yer teachin' school?"

"Naw, *goin'* ta school. College."

"Oh college." The tone in which he repeated what I'd said was ambiguous. Perhaps he was checking to see if he'd heard right, or maybe he was stalling until he could think of an appropriate response. I figured he probably disapproved of someone as old as I was still being in school and wondered why I wasn't married. I adjusted Lucera's tiedown so I wouldn't have to look directly at him. "Izzatright?" he beamed at me and pushed his hat back. "Now ain't that somethin'? Now that's jus' wonderful. You know there ain't nothin' like a' education. I only got through the sixth grade or so an' then I had ta go ta work. I ain't done bad, but you young folks cain't do without that schoolin' like we could. Well, you must be 'bout through college by now."

I had relaxed again in the warmth of his approval. Draping a coiled rope over my saddle horn, I informed him that actually I was sort of finished with college. "I'm in graduate school now," I explained, although even as I did so I wondered whether I might not be pushing my luck further than his enthusiasm for education could stretch. However, he still looked friendly and curious.

"Graduate school, huh?"

"Yeah, I'm workin' on a Ph.D."

"A P-H-D. I see. Well, so how much longer ya figurin' on bein' in school?" He paused briefly, tilted his chin up, and squinted his eyes. "How long ya *been* in school?" Oddly enough, nobody had ever asked me that question before, so I had to think.

"Altogether?"

"Yeah, altogether."

"Well, lessee, I'm 'bout twenty-eight years old, an' I been in school since I was six. Guess about twenty-two years." Mr. Ammons emitted a low whistle, as though he were mightily impressed. Gratified, I silently composed the requisite humble and self-effacing dismissal of my achievements.

"Damn, you musta been dumb when ya started," he said before I could air it. Then he grinned impishly.

I'd have gotten a bigger kick out of the old cowboy's sally if my father had not laughed so loudly and then gone to tell my mother about it immediately after Mr. Ammons had drifted to someone else's trailer. She got practically hysterical and was still chuckling as she made her way to the grandstands to watch the roping. I laughed too, of course, but the first loop I threw at a steer sailed a foot and a half beyond his horns and hit the ground. "You tryin' ta chop his head off? Don't swing so hard," my father instructed me as we both slowed our running horses and trotted out of the arena. Since his first "header" had missed too, he hadn't yet gotten to throw a heeling loop.

"I'm sorry I don' get ta practice three hours a day!" I bristled. "I'm in graduate school tryin' ta get over bein' so stupid, ya know." But he had already loped off to talk strategy with his next partner and didn't hear my apology.

After the roping was over, we unsaddled and cooled out the horses and then loaded them for the short trip to the ranch. My brother was in college and wouldn't be on vacation for another couple weeks, and my sister was married and came to the ropings with her husband and children. Therefore, only my parents and I were riding in the pickup, into which all five of us had used to pile for outings such as these. They chatted pleasantly, apparently not noticing my sour disposition. My mother said she was impressed that I'd caught as many steers as I had, since I never got a chance to practice. "I believe if you'd rope them at the north end instead of tracking them to the south end, ya'll might win something."

"I don't s'pose it matters much ta ya'll," I snapped, "but I'm in graduate school. I don' get much chance to practice. I'm *sorry* I can't rope 'em ta suit ya." I knew my mother had turned to look at me, so I kept my head ducked and stared at my knees. Nobody said anything more for a few minutes, but the dam had sprung a leak, so to speak, and there was nothing for it but that it drain entirely. "I get the *distinct* impression," I said, enunciating in an exaggeratedly precise way, "that neither of you cares doodley squat that I'm in graduate school. You don't ever ask me anything about what I do there." My knees, not used to being part of someone who spoke out so boldly, drew nervously closer to one another. "I just finished general exams, for heaven's sake. That's a big deal. My friends had a party for me. All you did was say 'honey, we're real proud of you. Did we tell you we'd bought a new horse?'"

My mother hesitated a moment, trying to gauge the depth of the chasm that had just opened between us, and then bravely ventured to cross it. "I thought you'd be interested in a new horse."

"I thought you'd be interested in my exams."

"We *are* interested. We just didn't realize they were so important, I guess."

"Ya'll wanna stop at Lakewood for a Coke?" my father interjected, shifting the gears of the big Chevy to slow down for a turn.

My outburst had an immediate and noticeable effect on my parents, who by the next morning had become elaborately polite. As she passed around the scrambled eggs, my mother asked if it were true that somebody besides Shakespeare had written Shakespeare's plays. She'd always wondered. I tried to answer in the same mode she'd asked—as though it were perfectly ordinary for us to have a little Shakespeare with our eggs.

"Oh, well," I said casually, spearing a strip of bacon with my fork, "some scholars theorize he wasn't educated enough to have written them." My father chewed his toast, stirred his coffee, and quietly asked for the salt, which my mother placed before him without removing her attentive eyes from my face. For some reason, I was embarrassed. "But thatsa buncha malarkey," I finished lamely, waving my hand to dismiss the topic and the scholars who had invented it. "Besides, there the plays are, and it doesn't matter who wrote 'em."

"That's kinda what I always thought," my mother nodded and then jumped up to get the coffee pot.

After my father finished his toast, he got up from the table and went into the living room to retrieve his hat, which he'd thrown on the floor beneath the hatrack, as he always did when he came in from the morning chores. He reentered the kitchen and, clamping the hat on his head, asked me if I'd help him fix the broken float on the water trough in the milk-cow pen. I was grateful for an excuse to get out of the kitchen, which seemed stuffy. I was also struck, however, by my father's manner. Customarily, he'd have said "Kathy Lynn, getcher gloves on and come help me fix that trough." I'd have said "what trough?" and he, rather than giving me a straight answer, would have pretended that my ignorance were unbearably provoking. "Whadaya mean 'what trough'? One that's been broken for the past week. Why would we wanna mess with any a' th' others?"

"I haven't been here for four months, in case you hadn't noticed," I'd have protested in the same sarcastic vein. "How 'm I s'posed ta know ya let the plumbin' go ta wrack an' ruin? You didn't tell me."

"You didn' ask."

But now, my father was being careful lest an awkward move tip my emotional canoe. "Sure," I replied jauntily to indicate that my load was still in balance, and then I followed him outside, feeling guilty about leaving my mother to do all the dishes but fairly certain she was relieved to have me go.

As we worked on the broken trough, my father's

behavior continued to be exemplary. Upon noticing that the bolt I was supposed to be holding still while he loosened the nut was turning in the jaws of my crescent wrench, he did not say "well, I got *my* wrench tuned up. Reckin we oughtta do this fer real now?" He just suggested, in the kindly way he reserved for helpless people not familiar with the subtle operations of crescent wrenches, that I reduce the size of the grip, and then he looked off toward the West Trap while I fumbled with the adjustment.

A couple of days later, when I forgot to lower the tailgate of the pickup before pulling away from the stock trailer I had just unhitched, he and my mother happened to be looking out the living room window. And, even though they actually witnessed the spectacle of the tailgate being ripped off its hinges by the trailer's arched "gooseneck," they still managed to be nice. "You know I almost did that myself the other day," my mother lied. "Been meanin' ta take that thing off anyway," muttered my father grimly after composing his features. "Pickup's s'posed ta get better gas mileage without it."

After about a week of their tender regard for my feelings, I was ready to pack my bags. I felt farther from home than I had a month earlier when I'd been sitting in a damp, cramped apartment reading *Confessions of an English Opium Eater*. I thought about telling my parents I had some work to do before school started again, but I had never left ahead of schedule before, and they'd undoubtedly misinterpret my doing so now as a "snit," which, given their efforts to be good, would bewilder and hurt them. I was trapped. Besides, my father had mentioned something about my mother and me helping him bring in a *corriente* steer and a couple of cows he'd seen at the river a day or two ago. "Ol' steer's kinda ornery about gettin' in the salt cedars," he had explained. Explaining things, never before his long suit, was part of his new policy toward me. "Last time I tried ta gather 'em, he swam the river an' I had the devil gettin' 'em back across." He had also suggested, tentatively, that I might like to try the new horse, a four-year-old registered dun quarterhorse named Dun Gone whom he had ridden several times and was beginning to think highly of. "He's still justa colt, but he's got lotsa cow sense," my father said. And the truth was, I was reluctant to leave without first getting my hands on the new horse.

Dun Gone was mettlesome and difficult to catch on the crisp morning we set out to hunt the steer and the cows. He snorted and whirled each time I drew near enough to touch his neck, and I finally had to trap him in a corner, where he stood with his tail turned toward me and his head thrust over the fence. Our horses were allowed their idiosyncrasies as long as these constituted no danger to us, but the youngster would have to be taught to "face," since a person walking past his hind quarters with the aim of reaching his head to put a bit in his mouth posed a temptation he might not always be trusted to resist. I didn't have time to fool with him right now though, so I made the perilous trek, talking to him all the while. "Whoa, Goner, whoa big knuckleheaded dummy," I whispered soothingly, holding out my hand and easing forward a step at a time. When I drew even with his flank, he "whuffed" and pushed against the fence with his chest as though he were trying to walk through it. I decided my guttural "ck" and hard "g" and "d" sounds had seemed threatening to him. You have to speak properly to a horse to win his confidence. I substituted for my initial epithets the more insinuating "silly-willy mutton sheep," whose fricatives and nasals had a calming influence. Or at least, as I carefully advanced past the powerful hind legs, continuing to offer my left hand for his inspection and to hold the bridle out of sight behind my back with the right, he did not offer to kick.

When he finally bent his neck around and blew nervously at my hand, his eyes wide and his nostrils flared, I scratched his nose with one finger, and then, since he stood for this imposition, I slowly inched my hand up the length of his head, passing over the white streak in his forehead and arriving at his ears, behind which I also scratched. Dun Gone sighed deeply when I massaged the spot between his ears, as though he were relieved to discover I was not going to brain him, and the tensions passed instantly out of his body. I knew I had him "caught." Slipping the reins around his neck to hold him while I bridled him was a mere formality. "That's a sweet silly-willy," I crooned, patting his neck. He was handsome and stockily built. My father had said he was well-broke and seemed intelligent, although he didn't know how to do anything yet. He had stopped trembling now and inquisitively smelled my hair as I led him to the saddle house.

The sun was up by the time we rode out of the waterlot toward the Pecos River, which wasn't very far from the house. In the bracing air, Dun Gone pranced and sidestepped, impatient at being held to a trot. My parents' more experienced horses saddlegaited matter-of-factly down the trail, conserving their energy. They had no idea how long their work day might last and wanted to save enough "gas" to get back home. Experience would teach Dun Gone not to work himself into a lather in the first half of the journey, as he had done this morning. "He's kind of an excitable little beast," my mother observed to my father after Dun Gone had danced another half mile. These were the first words any of us had spoken. We were absorbed in our own thoughts, breathing the crystalline air and unbuttoning our jackets as the sun blazed up. "Yeah, but he's bone gentle," my father assured her. "He jus' needs some ridin'."

Prolonged silences during horseback rides are not unusual—the rhythmic beat of the horses' hooves and the slight swaying of the body in the saddle are conducive to reverie and meditation—but I felt like talking and took advantage of my mother having broken the ice. Since I was not used to seeing her ride, I mentioned that she and Cajun, the horse my father had saddled for her, seemed to hit it off pretty well.

"I guess we should," she answered with a half smile. "I've ridden him a million miles." I was surprised by this revelation and asked her when she'd ever had a chance to do that. My mother's horseback outings had become less frequent as my brother and sister and I had grown older and "replaced" her. During big roundups, she generally drove the "chuckwagon," the pickup packed with pot roasts, beans, rolls, and cobblers, to the holding pens and fed the crew instead of riding. Now she looked quizzically at me, apparently bothered by something in the tone of my question.

"Well, I rode him three days straight when Hart and I gathered the yearlings out of High Lonesome and the Middle Pasture a couple of weeks ago. Before that, we hunted strays across the river for two days, and I rode him then. Before that, we got some cattle out of the forbidden zone." My father was trotting along in front of us with his free hand stuck in the hip pocket of his Levis, scanning the brush on either side of the trail for tracks. I rode beside my mother, making Dun Gone pick his way through the mesquite so that Cajun could stay on the narrow trail.

"So you're probably sick of 'em, not just used to 'em," I joked, trying to keep the conversation alive.

"Not really," my mother replied. I cast about for another topic and asked her what the "forbidden zone" was, figuring it was some "pet" name she and my father had invented to describe a piece of rough country somewhere.

"It's the four sections of the High Lonesome pasture the government just took out of our lease. They're going to build a dam," she said.

Stunned, I searched her face to see if she were serious. "They took four sections of High Lonesome?"

"Yep."

"How can they do that? They can't do that. I thought they couldn't afford to build any dams for awhile."

"They can do whatever they want to. The state and federal governments own all the land. You know that."

"But we've had that land in the lease since you bought the ranch. We can't afford to lose four sections. Which four?"

"That big tabosa flat with the windmill in it. They've fenced it off, and they've already bulldozed most of the grass. They call us whenever any of the cattle crawl back through the fence and tell us to come get them."

"That's the best part of the ranch." My mother remained silent, and my father veered off the trail to look more closely at some tracks. "When did this happen?"

"Oh, we've known they were going to do it for awhile. The fence got put up a couple of months ago." Until this point, my mother's voice had betrayed no emotion, as though she and my father had already gotten through the tangle of pain this amputation of the Heart-Diamond had undoubtedly caused them. But traces of bitterness crept in now. "The idiots spent a fortune building a fence and then didn't bother to run it all the way down the hill going off to the river in the southwest corner. They left a three-foot gap and a 'no trespassing' sign. The cows have a trail there. They don't read too well."

"How come you didn't tell me about this?" Before my mother could reply, my father pointed toward the river. A spotted steer and a little bevy of cows were grazing among some white boulders near a watering at the mouth of the draw down which we were riding. Most of the river bank was lined with salt cedars, but where the draw and the river converged, no trees grew, the grass was abundant, and water was easily accessible. The cattle threw up their heads and watched as we approached, but cooperatively set off up the draw toward the house when we started them, pausing every couple of yards to snatch "one last" mouthful.

I rode along behind them, herding them more or less automatically as I tried to fathom the sickening news my mother had just told me. There suddenly seemed to be many things I did not fully understand, including what the loss of the undulating sea of grass in High Lonesome—one-fifth of the Heart-Diamond—might mean to the future of the ranch, which barely supported itself as it was.

"You kinda need ta watch that ol' steer," I heard my father say, though his warning did not fully register. "He's gentle but he's a calculatin' ol' cuss." As if on cue, the steer meandered to the edge of the bunch of cows, wrapped his prehensile tongue around a clump of salt grass flourishing among the roots of a greasewood bush, pulled the grass into his mouth, and jerked his head up sharply to break the stems. Then, with several yellow strands dangling from his jaws, he nonchalantly leaped into a gully that ran the length of the draw and began to follow it back toward the river at a brisk trot.

I came out of my trance. I had forgotten about the gully, a notorious escape route, but now remembered that it passed through the salt cedars and went all the way to the river. Before it got that far, however, it wound its way through a dense patch of brush. By the time Dun Gone negotiated the brush, the steer would have reached the cedars and probably crossed the river. My best chance to get him back would be to ride down into the gully myself, catch up with him, and then dash past him and turn him at the first place the narrow channel widened enough to permit it. Unfortunately, he had a pretty good head start.

And not altogether surprisingly, Dun Gone balked when I asked him to slide down the steep embankment, although his instinctive "cow sense" told him we should get around the steer. He threw his ears forward and dropped his nose to the ground to inspect the point where the steer's tracks went off, reluctantly edging forward when I tapped him with the end of a rein and touched him with my spurs. When I tapped him again, he bunched his body, drawing his hind quarters under him as though he were preparing to leap the gully (a feat he could not perform and the attempt of which would probably kill both of us), so I stopped "crowding" him. I hated the idea of being outfoxed by the steer, whose horns I could see disappearing around a bend. Nevertheless, I let Dun Gone teeter uncertainly on the brink of the deep gully until he made up his mind he could do what I asked of him, whereupon, half jumping and half sliding, he went down amid a shower of dirt and small stones.

As we raced along the rocky corridor, I kept an eye on the steer's tracks. I didn't think he could climb back up the five-foot embankment until he got into the cedars, but I was wrong. A few yards before the gully entered the trees, it widened and grew shallower, and a trail, picking its way down the west bank, crossed and went up the east bank toward the foothills above, where it continued to parallel the river. Sure enough, the steer, in what I considered to be a strategic error, had followed the trail out, as his tracks testified. I followed the tracks, knowing I could get around the steer once we had topped out in the country above the river.

For the first ten yards of the relatively easy ascent, the trail was smooth. I urged the colt along, trying to draw close enough to the steer to see him. I could hear him climbing ahead of me where the trail went around the edge of the hill. He knocked loose small rocks and gravel, which rattled down toward the cedars, as he went. I got high enough to see the Pecos over the thin row of trees lining its banks. It was a sparkling green ribbon woven among the dry hills; when you thought about it, it struck you as a miraculous presence in this arid landscape. Dun Gone responded eagerly, as though he were trying to make up for the time he had cost us.

Then we reached the section of the trail that leveled off and followed the contours of the hill where it swelled outward toward the river. Dun Gone spooked a little, hesitated, stutter-stepped another couple of yards, and stopped, trembling, to peer over the edge. I should have given him time. If I had, he'd have found his way. But I could see the steer now, trotting insolently ahead of us, so I spurred the colt, forgetting in my impatience that he could easily outrun the "renegade" in the flat country above. I had let the steer escape and was determined to bring him back.

Instead of picking up the pace when I asked him, Dun Gone, suddenly terrified, tried to whirl and go back the way he had come. At any other point on the trail, he might have had room to execute the maneuver. But where he tried it (and of course he tried it there for the very reasons that made it impossible), the trail narrowed, the hill above it jutted out sharply, and the drop toward the river, though not sheer, grew appreciably steeper. Not believing he could traverse the thin ledge that ran around the outcropping, Dun Gone reared slightly and pivoted toward the hill on his hind legs, encountering a rocky protuberance with his front ones. His back feet slipped off the trail into loose dirt that cascaded down the slope as it gave way under his weight. Maybe if he had kept his head or if I had kept mine, we'd have gotten ourselves out of the fix we were suddenly in. But he, in his terror, tried to complete the turn, while I, unable to quell my own rising panic, tried to pull his head back around. Soon we found ourselves in the early, "slow-motion" stage of a tumble off the hill. I heard my father shout just at the instant I could feel, from the position of my body, that the colt could not possibly regain his balance.

The first part of the fall really was in slow motion because Dun Gone spent two or three seconds trying to lunge back onto the trail. Adrenalin flooded my chest and made my heart pump so fiercely it ached. I glanced over my shoulder and saw the cedars and the river below. A simple fall down the slope might not hurt me, but I did not think I could survive the crushing weight of a nine hundred pound horse rolling over me several times while I did it, especially if the saddle horn were to catch me in the chest or the stomach. I had had numerous "wrecks" on horses, but none had ever presented to me so stark a picture of my vulnerability and fragility as this one now did.

I was starting to lose my seat and clawed at Dun Gone's mane for a handhold, leaning forward over the saddle horn even as the colt's head rose in the air. He was going off slightly sideways, so that I hung on a second or two longer than I could have if he had come straight over backwards. Instinctively, I gripped the thick black mane with both hands, lifted my legs up to his rump, and tried to haul myself forward onto his neck to push his head down, but the angle was already too severe, and my weight merely contributed to the forces pulling him over. Yet I still clung desperately.

During the next few degrees of the arc through which we were falling, my mind grew preternaturally calm, like the eye in the center of a hurricane. More accurately, it seemed to be suspended in the air just beyond the periphery of the accident and to be observing with a detached, problem-solving interest. Although my fingers still scrabbled in Dun Gone's mane, my brain absorbed with uncharacteristic speed and efficiency the relevant data and concluded, quite at odds with my body, that I must do exactly the opposite of what I was doing; that is, instead of hanging to the horse and being under him when he fell, I had to get as far from him as possible—try to make it down the hill ahead of the flailing hooves, the dilated nostrils and eyes, the dull thud of the muscular frame hitting the earth, bouncing, hitting again, the flowing black mane. But I could not make myself let go until all at once an inrushing fear of being crushed to death drove out the fear of falling. Instinct caught up with reason and I jumped the only way I could, backwards, pushing off from the horse with both hands to open up a gap between us, and dropping blindly through space.

I fell toward the river and the trees. Time sped up now, and I did not fall "forever." Rather, the ground slammed into me instantly, knocking the air out of my lungs. I was unprepared for the severity of the blow—for the sensation that my bones, and especially my spine, were no longer encased in protective, shock-absorbing flesh. Still, I was not aware of any particular pain, just of the numbing effects of landing flat on my back. I supposed that maybe my wild trip was already over but then felt myself turning a violent backward somersault and another and another. Foremost in my mind, however, was the image of Dun Gone overtaking me—of his shod hooves hitting the back of my head and his massive weight breaking every bone in my body. If I could have made myself turn faster, I would have.

Finally I stopped rolling, but I was even more frightened than I had been up on the trail or careening down the hill, for even though I was no longer moving, Dun Gone surely was. I could hear his grunts and the noise of dislodged pebbles and dirt, so I did not pause to take stock of my injuries but began to crawl, like a maimed insect, first one direction and then another. I had lost my glasses and could not see very well, but mainly I had lost my bearings and had no idea from which quadrant Dun Gone's hurtling form would strike me. Then I became aware that I was among the cedars and crawled furiously toward the river until my hands and knees were in water. After that,

I quit crawling and lay face down, covering the back of my head with my hands as I'd been taught to do anytime a horse fell with me. I propped my face out of the water with my elbows and waited. The river stank like dead fish.

It didn't dawn on me right away as I lay there that I was hearing nothing except the gentle lapping of the river against its banks. I remained still, listening, making certain the colt was no longer after me, although common sense should have told me he couldn't still be falling after all this time. Finally, I sat up and noticed that my clothes were soaked and covered with black ooze, that my glasses were gone, and that my limbs, though limp, were all intact. Various internal connections seemed to have been momentarily disrupted, but slowly, the signals sorted themselves out, and I got myself onto the dry bank.

I did not wonder yet what had become of Dun Gone. What came to mind next were the faces of my parents as I had seen them, or imagined I'd seen them, when the horse had begun to lose his balance. They had come back to help me, supposing I had let the steer get to the cedars, and had ridden up the trail just in time to see my theatrical accident. I had a distinct impression of their mouths opening in ineffectual shouts. I recalled a look that had come over my mother's face once when a doctor had entered a hospital waiting room to report on the condition of my sister, who had fallen off her horse and struck her head on a rock. I had not been old enough at the time to understand that my sister might die and knew only that something terrible had shattered my parents' confidence and strength. I imagined them sitting in that same speechless horror up above, searching the cedars for any signs of movement.

Touching a spot on my forehead that had begun to

throb, I started to shout as loudly as I could, "I'm okay, I'm okay, I'm okay," my voice cracking with emotion as I realized I *was* okay. I patted the mud around me trying to locate my glasses, shouting and crying as I searched, and at last saw the gleam of their gold frames at the roots of one of the cedars farthest from the river. For some reason, perhaps because I still felt shaky, I crawled to them rather than standing up. After bending them back into a semblance of their original shape, I put them on and looked up at the ledge, but my parents weren't there. I was afraid they still might not know what had become of me, so I cried out, louder than before, "I'm not hurt, I'm not hurt."

A mustard-colored blotch caught at the corner of my right eye and caused me to break off midsentence. Dun Gone lay stretched out in a thicket of catclaw and mesquite that grew at the base of the incline we had just come down. I must have passed through it without noticing the thorns. It occurred to me that I had also managed to roll among the trunks of the cedars without hitting one, a piece of luck Dun Gone, by virtue of his much larger size, wouldn't have shared if he'd gotten that far. I had been more or less safe the moment I had entered the sanctuary of the cedars. It was odd that the horse had been stopped by the brush when I hadn't, but there he lay with his head pointing up the hill. I did not yell anymore.

My parents came crashing out of the cedars left of and a little behind me, and I thought how ridiculous it had been for me to suppose they had just sat on their horses awaiting the outcome of the fall. Of course they had dismounted and slid down a less precipitous part of the hill and then dodged and scrambled through the fringe of trees along the bank until they had reached me. I gazed up at them through my bent frames, and, for a second or two, we communicated in that mute language that is the merging of souls, momentarily purged of their superficial differences by the scalding heat of fear and love. Then I saw the tension flow out of the muscles of their faces, and we found, once again, our old voices. "Scared ya, didn't I!?" I asked, grinning wryly.

"Not 'til ya started all that caterwaulin'," replied my father. "Did ya let that ol' steer get away?"

My mother helped me to my feet and lifted up my shirt to inspect my back, which I could feel was scraped, while my father went over to inspect Dun Gone. He stood at the colt's head gazing down at him.

"He's dead, isn't he?" I asked miserably.

"Don't you wish!" said my father. "I prob'ly oughtta slit 'is throat right now while it 'ud be so easy. Dun Gone, you li'l idjit, whadaya think yer doin' down there?" The colt switched his tail. "He's got his headstall hung over a mesquite root and he cain't get up . . . can ya silly wit?"

Dun Gone was not struggling. Apparently he had determined some while back that he couldn't help himself, so he was waiting calmly to be helped. My father talked quietly to him as he disentangled the headstall and then pulled him to his feet. The colt seemed to have come away from the fall unscathed except for a bleeding knee and a raw spot over one eye.

"He's not a silly wit," I said, "I am. I shoulda had better sense than to ride 'em up that trail when he didn't want to go."

"Oh, well," my mother responded, "we thought maybe you were teaching him how to fly. Looked like he might learn there for a second or two, but I guess his design's not quite right."

"He flies okay if ya don' mind upside down," rejoined

my father. "He jus' doesn't know how ta land yet." With a violent shake, Dun Gone rid himself of the memory of his ordeal.

"Maybe we better let her go back to the house," my mother suggested, pulling my shirt back down. "She's prob'ly gonna get pretty sore."

"Oh, she doesn't need ta go ta the house," he replied in his "irritated" voice. "Sore never hurt anybody. Besides, she's gonna spoil my steer if she lets 'em get away again."

Dun Gone lifted his nose high in the air, yawned cavernously, and then nickered at the other horses to find out where they'd gotten themselves off to. I led him as we all walked back through the cedars and climbed the hill together.